FINDING THE ALPENGLOW

FINDING THE ALPENGLOW

MY JOURNEY TO STABILITY WHILE LIVING WITH BIPOLAR DISORDER

KATE ARREDONDO

NEW DEGREE PRESS

COPYRIGHT © 2021 KATE ARREDONDO

All rights reserved.

FINDING THE ALPENGLOW

MY JOURNEY TO STABILITY WHILE LIVING WITH

BIPOLAR DISORDER

ISBN   978-1-63730-705-2   *Paperback*

            978-1-63730-796-0   *Kindle Ebook*

            979-8-88504-010-5   *Ebook*

To my parents, for loving me no matter what.
To my husband, for being my best friend
and my rock.
To my daughter, for giving me unwavering strength.
To my brother, for saving me.
To my sister, for always listening to me.

To anyone with a mental illness, for enduring.

CONTENTS

INTRODUCTION		1
CHAPTER 1.	HOW I GOT HERE	5
CHAPTER 2.	MUSIC FOR MY SOUL	17
CHAPTER 3.	MY PILLARS OF SUPPORT	29
CHAPTER 4.	THE SHIFT	39
CHAPTER 5.	YOU REALLY ARE WHAT YOU EAT	47
CHAPTER 6.	THE MARATHON	55
CHAPTER 7.	GET SOME REST	63
CHAPTER 8.	THE RELEASE	71
CHAPTER 9.	FOOTPRINTS ON MY HEART	81
CHAPTER 10.	A CHANGE OF PACE	95
CHAPTER 11.	MOTHER NATURE	101
CHAPTER 12.	THAT LITTLE VOICE INSIDE	107
CHAPTER 13.	DAILY RITUALS	119
CHAPTER 14.	THE KEY: MIND, BODY & SPIRIT	129
ACKNOWLEDGEMENTS		135
APPENDIX		139

INTRODUCTION

I was driving to work when the panic hit. My lips curled down in despair, quivering. Tears welled in my eyes, and suddenly my breath was short and troubled. Snot began filling my sinuses and running down my nose. I was gasping for air.

I was sleep deprived. I was in survival mode. I was tapering down from exclusively pumping for my thirteen-month-old daughter. All the while, surviving in a job I felt had no purpose.

It had been almost ten years since I had an attack like this. I called my mom, one of two people who can calm me down when I lose control. She always listens—while holding space for me to recognize the flawed thinking that wound me up in the first place. After I was able to finally regain my breath on the phone with her, we agreed it was time to reach out to my psychiatrist and update her on my panic attack.

I had been off my medications for bipolar disorder for over two years, a decision I made with both my psychiatrist and my husband so that we could start our family.

My medication had a risk for congenital disabilities and over the last five years, I had been able to taper my therapeutic dose down by half with no major episodes. So, when my husband and I met with my psychiatrist before trying to have a baby, she felt confident that with the help of pregnancy hormones, I could completely taper off my medications over six months and still be able to maintain my mental stability during pregnancy and breastfeeding. That is the beautiful thing about a woman's body: it will do anything in its power to protect the baby.

While the pregnancy hormones had been sufficient in keeping me stable over the last twenty-two months, my levels were returning to normal as I weaned from breast pumping. I wasn't utilizing the few coping mechanisms I knew, let alone making a plan for the transition to life unmedicated. All I knew was that I was desperate not to go back on my medications. I had come this far and refused to accept that I was not *emotionally strong enough (my ever-present gremlin message)* to control my mood without medication.

The Shift

Over the next three years, I would discover simple yet powerful resources and utilize them to bring balance to my life. I was embarking on a spiritual awakening, a journey that would bring a complete shift in my mindset and allow me to go from coping to thriving with my illness.

The Centers for Disease Control and Prevention's website on mental health states that more than 264 million people suffer from depression globally, with eight hundred thousand dying from suicide each year. In our country alone, one in every twenty-five Americans lives with a serious mental illness, such as schizophrenia, bipolar disorder, or major depression. Additionally, it was found that 1 in every 5 Americans will experience a mental illness each year, (CDC, 2021).

What's even more alarming, though, is the stigma around mental illness, which can make it harder for those suffering to reach out for help. Our society superficially considers people with mental illnesses as "crazy." Common stereotypes make it seem like someone with a mental illness will never be stable, successful, happy, or have a family of their own.

When I first began struggling with my mental illness in high school, I fell victim to these fears. I did not want to be seen as "crazy," so I kept my dark thoughts to myself and made excuses for why I could not go out with my friends. I quit the sports I loved and hid in my bedroom. I felt unequipped to handle the mental marathon that comes with having a mental illness, and the self-induced isolation further intensified my suffering.

After that fateful panic attack driving to work, I went back to my psychiatrist and started learning about meditation and mindfulness. In my search for answers on living a more purposeful life, I discovered an interview with Nik Wood on the podcast, Energy Matters, that introduced me to life coaching. It inspired me to become a certified professional coach. My yearlong coach training program at the Institute for Professional Excellence in Coaching (iPEC) allowed me to connect with my true self and taught me how to move from a victim mindset to one of endless opportunities.

At the time of writing, it has been three and a half years since I first learned about meditation from my psychiatrist after my panic attack. My mental illness is no longer my weakness; it is my superpower. It has given me the awareness, courage, and strength to weather any storm. I understand now that I am in control. My thoughts do not define me; my mood does not define me. I have learned many incredible life lessons from my spiritual journey. They have helped me go from merely coping to fully thriving in my life. I want to share my experiences with you so that you, too, may develop hope that life can, and will, be better.

Your life matters. You can *choose to live*—no matter how bad you feel or how much you do not want to at this moment in time. You *are* worth it. You have the power to thrive in your life. Every second that passes is an *opportunity for a restart*. We only ever have the *present moment* to choose our new course.

Medication and therapy will always play a vital role in your mental health journey. I will guide you through the experiences and lessons that I have learned to help keep myself grounded and maintain long-lasting mental stability. By nourishing your mind, body, and soul, you can develop your own unique recipe for stability.

My mental health recipe is a mixture of things everyone has available for use at any time, in varying degrees, depending on the moment. The good news is that the tools are simple. We all have exceptional minds that give us the ability to reframe our thoughts and gain control of our struggles with mental health in order to find our purpose in life.

> "Your present circumstances do not
> determine where you can go; they
> merely determine where you start."
>
> —NIDO QUBEIN

CHAPTER 1

HOW I GOT HERE

———

"The only journey is the journey within."

—RAINER MARIA RILKE

"Middle school was the best time of my life," said no one ever. That is where my mental health journey began, sixth grade, to be exact.

Up until that point, I had attended a small private school in Austin, Texas called Kirby Hall, from kindergarten through to fifth grade. My class had consisted of thirteen classmates from various backgrounds, races, and religions. I had classmates from Africa, Iran, and England and teachers from Spain and Germany. I had no concept that the color of someone's skin meant anything "different" about them at all. We were all extremely close and had been secluded from societal pressures in our blue and white uniforms and safely kept in a three-story, red-brick bubble.

Starting in the first grade, we learned Spanish and German, along with advanced mathematics and sciences. There was a computer lab with first-generation teal and white Apple iMacs, and we were given dedicated weekly learning time to use them. We also learned to play musical instruments of our choosing.

Kirby Hall was my little utopia, but there was just one thing missing. My parents knew that I had an interest in sports and felt that it was time for me to have the opportunity to join sports teams. Since that wasn't an option at my private school, my parents decided it was time for me to attend public school.

Middle School

I started my sixth-grade year at Dripping Springs Middle School. To say this was an adjustment is a vast understatement.

I suddenly felt lost in a group of 350-plus students—99 percent white—full of cliques and trends I did not understand. I had no idea what designer clothing brands were, let alone which ones were in or out. I had never owned a pair of Doc Martens or Gap overalls. I had grown up listening to oldies and Elvis in my parents' car, not Backstreet Boys or the Spice Girls.

I greatly struggled to find friends during that first year. I quickly learned the cruel truth about preteens and how mean they really can be to each other. I came home from school crying almost every day, wondering why my new classmates were so hurtful. I didn't know what I was doing wrong for them to treat me that way. This transition changed me from an innocent, sociable girl to a sad, quiet recluse.

Looking back, this was the first time my mental health had spiraled.

In an effort to help me make some friends, my parents enrolled me in basketball at the local youth sports association since team athletics didn't start until seventh grade. I had a natural talent for basketball. It became my respite from school, and I became friends with a couple of girls on the team.

In seventh grade, I tried out and made the "A" team for basketball, and as an athlete, I began to find my place in the pecking order amongst my fellow teenagers. My teammates helped me to feel valuable again. I found reprieve from the isolation and teasing I had experienced in sixth grade. Basketball and the overall team environment were healing for my mind, body, and soul.

High School

One day during practice in my junior year, we were running a press defense drill, and I was about to cross the half-court mark (where the defenders were supposed to drop off). As I approached half-court, hugging the sideline while dribbling the ball, I got cut off by a defender. I had been hastily attempting to beat her to the line, but suddenly, I found myself flying through the air. I landed, my knee striking a metal plate in the floor off-court.

I pushed my upper body off the ground as my coach asked if I was okay. I did not feel any pain, so I stood myself back up. I took a step and was surprised; I immediately collapsed to the hard gym floor. My stomach seemed to somersault. A teammate reached out a hand and hauled me to my feet again, but tears were already streaming down my face. Dark, icy fear gripped my chest.

I was determined it was not going to be the end of my junior season. I struggled for several weeks with the injury as the school trainer felt I only needed ice and muscle stimulating therapy to recover. I was desperate to be able to play again. The regular season was coming to an end, and we were expected to make it to the state tournament again. We even had a good chance at winning it.

After weeks of resting my knee and not practicing, it still didn't feel any better. My parents became concerned about the trainer's diagnosis and insisted upon an orthopedist appointment. After having an MRI, it was confirmed I had a partially torn posterior cruciate ligament (PCL). I was told, even with surgery, it could potentially cause more harm than good. Time and rehabilitation were recommended; surgery was not.

It was unlike the usual ACL or MCL injuries commonly found in basketball; they are extremely painful, causing massive amounts of swelling, followed by corrective surgery and almost complete recovery with a knee brace. I, however, constantly walked around feeling unstable, as if I could not trust my knee to hold my body weight. I remember my doctor explaining that the PCL is normally considered the strongest ligament of the knee, usually being the only ligament to remain intact after a total blowout.

The orthopedist advised that I no longer participate in the track and field events in which I had excelled (high jump and hurdles), as a simple misstep or twist could easily result in a total knee blowout. Playing basketball would now always require a knee brace, and I would need to constantly keep my upper leg muscles strong to avoid my leg from overcompensating. I began physical therapy and finished that season watching my team from the bench. We lost by a point with a last-second shot—in only the regional game.

I entered my senior year feeling better about my injury and more comfortable wearing my brace. I even had a few colleges still interested in recruiting me. Then, one practice at the very start of the season, we performed a new defensive drill designed to block the ball with the backside of our hand as it is being passed between offensive players. During my third turn intercepting the pass, my hand struck the ball, and I felt a sharp, stabbing pain in my thumb.

Again, I knew it was not going to be the season I had imagined.

My coach was hesitant to believe my fears that my thumb was broken. I went straight to the locker room and called my dad. I told him I was certain I had just broken my thumb in practice. As soon as those words left my lips, I broke down, crying hysterically on the locker room floor.

The following morning, I headed to the orthopedist again, completely devastated. The X-ray revealed I had a break vertically down the middle bone in my right thumb, starting at the middle joint. I was put in a hard cast and told that I would need at least six weeks to heal. I immediately felt a glimmer of hope because I would still be able to play the last half of my senior year.

In my first practice back, after getting the cast removed, I went up for a rebound and was met with another player's hand, reaching for the ball but finding my thumb instead. The next thing I knew, I was lying on the basketball court looking up, surrounded by my coach and fellow teammates. I had passed out from the pain of my re-injury.

It was then that I knew *it was over. My dream was gone.*

I was crushed—and a few weeks later, I quit the team.

So much of the last two years of high school have now disappeared into a black hole of memories. I know now that was due to disassociation. My psychiatrist has since explained that this is the brain's attempt to protect itself during mental trauma by disconnecting itself from memories.

My emotions became erratic. I often cried and let paranoia about my friendships push me to isolation. What was supposed to be the most exciting time had turned into the biggest disappointment.

Seeing my mental state deteriorate over my senior year, my mother tried as hard as she could to get me the help I needed after I quit basketball. Unfortunately, it resulted in being misdiagnosed—first with ADHD, then with depression, and even by a psychologist who thought a Myers-Briggs personality test and hypnotherapy would cure me.

Despite my knee injury and leaving the team, I had accepted a basketball scholarship with Trinity University in San Antonio before graduation. Being a division-three level, it was not the type of scholarship I had been expecting, but I was happy with the fact that I would get a second chance at my basketball career. It gave me some sense of hope for my future.

College

The summer after graduating from high school, my behavior became reckless and self-destructive. I would sneak out of my parents' house at night and go to underage parties to binge drink alcohol. I couldn't bring myself to start the summer basketball conditioning schedule I had been given by the coach, despite my dad's constant reminders. The summer flew by in a haze of mania and drunkenness—in an attempt to suppress my emotions.

By the end of July, I began even struggling to wake up most mornings. I had a surge of anxiety about the changes coming in the next month and, in my trepidation, decided I did not want to play basketball anymore.

I arrived at Trinity University in August for orientation week. I was full of fear, terrified of being around new people and a new environment. I arrived at my empty dorm room, where my mom and I unpacked my things. I then found out that my assigned roommate was not coming. Having settled in, I finally mustered up the strength to call and speak to my coach, letting him know I would not be playing that season. A few hours later, a group of senior members from the team came to my door to welcome me. I quickly dismissed them, retreating to my bed and only leaving it for assigned school orientation activities.

A few days later, I was reassigned a roommate who would be arriving from out of the country. Forced with the concept of having to share my space with a complete stranger, I became desperate and called my mom. I pleaded with her that I wanted to go home and that I was not going to stay at college. She tried to comfort me and asked that I give it more time. I was adamant that I wanted nothing but to leave. She drove to my dorm and had me speak with my resident assistant.

They tried desperately to convince me to change my decision and pleaded with me to stay and try it out. I remember becoming hysterical, and my mom attempted to find me a doctor to talk to on campus. After obtaining a medical withdrawal, we packed up my things, and I went home.

The next few months back at home are even more of a black hole in my memory. I laid in bed for days on end, only getting up to shower every few days—but only after constant pleading from my mother. I barely ate, mostly slept, and got yelled at often by my father. He did not understand anything that was going on with me and thought I should be able to just "snap" out of it. Even my mother, a medically trained doctor, had no experience with someone struggling with mental health.

Luckily, my mom finally received a recommendation for a psychiatrist. I went to my first appointment, my mother by my side. The office was a large corner room with floor-to-ceiling windows on two sides. Dr. Hauser had invited us to sit on a dark red couch in the middle of the room accented with an embroidered Boston Terrier pillow. She handed both of us a questionnaire to fill out and then had us each share my history with her. After reflecting for a few minutes, Dr. Hauser had diagnosed me with Bipolar Type II Disorder and Social Anxiety Disorder.

She also explained that my previous misdiagnosis had caused my condition to worsen. Being treated for one disease or the other, not the underlying problem, contributed to harsher cycles between mania and depression. She then laid out her plan, which would start with a low-dose mood stabilizer, Lamictal, and told me to wait a few weeks before I'd begin to feel better.

It was the first sense of relief that I had received in a long time. Finally, I felt a flicker of hope inside my chest, thanks to Dr. Hauser's thorough understanding of my situation.

Within three or four weeks of taking Lamictal, I felt some relief. The constant black clouds I seemed to never be able to escape had turned grey with a glimmer of sun peeking through.

Months went by, and I felt significantly better. So much so, I even decided to re-enroll in university at Texas State and give college another try. I completed the summer semester while staying on campus in a dorm room on my own and then decided to get an apartment near the school for the upcoming fall semester. I felt I was back on track.

By the spring semester of the following year, I knew I had control of my mind again. I overconfidently believed that it all must have been a phase. *Did I even need medication anymore?* Taking my medication was a downer and would put me in a state of drowsiness. I could barely stay awake in class. *I must not need it anymore.* Dr. Hauser offered to switch me to a new mood stabilizer to see if the drowsiness would decrease. I took the new medication for a few weeks but decided I hated it. I then quit taking any of my medication.

I didn't tell anyone.

What's the worst that could happen?

Things spiraled downward rapidly, and I found myself desperately trying to act like everything was fine.

It wasn't.

Not only had I quit my medication, but I also quit my schoolwork and stopped attending class. The "darkness" became harder and harder to fight—and I soon succumbed to it. Once again, I reached out to my mother to save me. She drove down, packed me up, and moved me back home again. I withdrew from college for the second time.

I spent the next eight months enduring the darkest part of my life. Reluctant to go back on Lamictal, I tried several different mood stabilizers and even experienced Lithium poisoning as a result. Nothing seemed to work, and my suicidal thoughts were turning into plans and actions. I just wanted my suffering to end. The only way I saw that happening was to end my life.

I had come up with several different options but settled upon the idea of driving my beloved Mustang Bullitt as fast as I could, straight into a tree. I snuck out of my room that night, got in my car, tears streaming down my face, my shirt soaked from snot. My mind was swarmed with questions. *What road should I do it on? What tree would it end up being?* Each thought brought more and more hopelessness. I felt there was no way out.

While on a back road, north of Dripping Springs, the sudden image of my five-year-old brother consumed my entire being. My front tires had just begun to leave the pavement, heading straight towards a big oak tree.

Our age gap of thirteen years made him feel more like a child than a brother to me. We were extremely close. *How would he feel waking up and being told I had killed myself?* I pictured his devastated face. He would be so confused. *None of this was his fault.*

I jerked the wheel back and slammed on the brakes as the car slid into the ditch, to a stop. I wondered, *How could I do this to him?*

I sat there, my hands desperately gripping the steering wheel, the car radio still blaring in the silence of the night. The smell of burnt rubber and smoke filled the air. Terrified of what I had almost done, I put the car in gear, floored the gas to get back onto the road, and sped home. His love for me, and mine for him, saved me.

Time continued on, but I still felt desperate to end my feelings of despair. I remember being literally dragged to the car one morning to go see my psychiatrist. When I arrived, she gave me an ultimatum: I could either agree to try Lamictal again or choose to be hospitalized and undergo electric shock therapy.

I was out of options, and I had a critical decision to make. My psychiatrist reiterated her hesitation to hospitalize me and told me it would not be a pleasant experience. Reluctantly, I agreed to restart the medication and work up to a therapeutic dose again.

Within several weeks, the light seemed to be returning. More months passed, and I woke up one morning with the strangest thought:

I am me again! I am Kate.

It was as if I had been trapped away, locked up in the darkest tower of my brain, only being allowed to observe from behind an invisible prison wall.

I had endured.

CHAPTER 2

MUSIC FOR MY SOUL

"Music washes away from the soul
the dust of everyday life."

—BERTHOLD AUERBACH

When I was about ten years old, we took a family vacation to the Great Smoky Mountains in Tennessee. The day before returning home, we decided to walk the local town and shop for souvenirs. There was a lovely gift shop on the main street with a log exterior and a green metal roof. Upon entering the store, my nose was overwhelmed with scents of pine and cinnamon. There were candles, books, jewelry, home décor, a sizable t-shirt section, and a kid's area to explore.

I looked around the store for a while but kept finding myself drawn to a CD sampler machine, where two other children were fighting over whose turn it was to put on the headphones. Eventually, they lost interest, and I took the opportunity to see what I had been missing.

I put the headphones on and noticed there were various buttons to preview different CDs. I began pressing the plastic buttons in sequential order, spending a few seconds listening to each one. I was suddenly intrigued when one button started playing a symphony of soft yet powerful tones of percussion, pipes, and keyboard. There were soft vocals in a foreign language that danced around the different octaves. This was my first introduction to Enya's *Shepherd Moons*.

I grabbed the CD from the bin and headed to meet my mom and sister by the cash register. Upon seeing my choice, my mother expressed her concern about me selecting something I could buy anywhere. She asked if I wanted to keep looking around. I was adamant that I had found what I wanted and even offered to pay for it with my allowance. She conceded, and as soon as we got back to the car, I popped the CD into my portable CD player and listened to it on the drive back to the cabin.

The Healing Power of Music

There was something about the resonance of Enya's voice, mixed with the sounds of the keyboard and various other instruments, that brought about a deep calm to the core of my body. Similar in sensation to moments when I am surrounded by nature while hiking in the Colorado mountains. It's a sense of connectedness to the Whole and being present in just that moment.

When I think about how I've relied on Enya's music throughout my life, it makes sense that whenever my depressive episodes swing back around, I find myself playing her music. I am able to put my headphones on and temporarily enter a space where the dark thoughts and feelings recede, and an almost trance-like state of serenity sweeps over me.

It does not matter if I am in a full-blown panic attack or if I have been sobbing uncontrollably. At the very least, I can close my eyes and let the music soothe me to sleep. Even now, after having been stable for over a decade, Enya can still bring about a calmness in me that is unmatched.

Norah Jones' song "Come Away with Me" had a similar meditative effect on me over the years. I usually played Norah Jones whenever I was upset and driving. I know; "upset" and "driving" should not be used in the same sentence. However, I made an exception for my beautiful, forest-green Mustang Bullitt, with an all-black leather interior and bucket seats that cradled my body. I felt one with the road whenever I downshifted and hugged the curves around the country back roads of Dripping Springs.

Norah's voice brought back some sense of feeling to me—a sort of therapeutic connection between Norah Jones, the car, and myself. What soothed me was the fact that I had control over every movement that the car made. I could choose where I wanted to go and how fast to do it. It was a feeling I did not have in my own life at that time.

A few years ago, I found myself searching for a new type of music to accompany my everyday activities. I had exchanged the darkness and sadness for stress and burnout. In a search on Spotify one day for a mindfulness playlist, I found one that featured an artist with whom I was unfamiliar: Andrew Belle.

As with Enya, there is not a song that Andrew sings that I do not love. His voice is soft and soothing, complemented by piano and strong drumbeats. His playlist makes an appearance pretty much every day, especially during the work week.

I feel his music deeply, at what I can only describe as being on a spiritual level. Maybe it's that Enya, Norah, and Andrew's voices are all soft tones, each with piano as the main accompaniment. It could be the rhythmic patterns or tempo of the beat. Maybe it's deeper than that. Regardless, whether with Enya, Norah, or Andrew, music plays an essential role in my ability to maintain my mood and overall mental stability. I consider it a staple in anyone's journey out of the darkness and into the light.

Music's Effect on the Brain

"Musical emotions and musical memory can survive long after other forms of memory have disappeared," stated Dr. Oliver Sacks, a British neurologist, in the *Psychology Today* article "Music, Emotion and Wellbeing," written by Dr. Shahram Heshmat. "Part of the reason for the durable power of music appears to be that listening to music engages many parts of the brain, triggering connections and creating associations," (Heshmat, 2019). That may explain why I, so many years later, still get the overwhelming sense of calm when I hear Enya's music, even when I'm feeling stable.

In the article, Dr. Heshmat also references a study by Matthew E. Sachs, a post-doctoral fellow at Columbia University. The study evaluated participants' emotional reactions to six pieces of music, three from their personal library and three control pieces. The findings showed that "people who consistently respond emotionally to aesthetic musical stimuli possess stronger white matter connectivity between their auditory cortex and the areas associated with emotional processing," (Heshmat, 2019).

This discovery means that when I listen to my playlists, I am actually increasing my brain's ability to process my current emotional state, as the music has activated and intensified that part of my temporal lobe.

Jim Donovan, a musician turned music professor at Saint Francis University, has devoted his career in higher education to understanding how the power of music can elevate our moods. In his interview "How Music Helps You Heal" on the meditation and mindfulness-based podcast *Untangle*, Jim describes his childhood experience learning firsthand the powerful healing effects of music.

Growing up in a low-income family, Jim found refuge in his early teenage years playing air drums on his bed with a pair of stolen drumsticks from his high school band hall. Drumming to AC/DC and Led Zeppelin vinyl records was a therapeutic way to release his teenage frustration. Donovan said, "from age 13 to 16, I sat there and just played. My mother would peek in the room sometimes to make sure I was still alive, and then she'd see that I was going to town playing in the air," (Karpas, 2020).

For fifteen years, Jim played in the band Rusted Root. His band opened for the Grateful Dead, Dave Mathews, Santana, and Jewel, to name a few. Over the years, Jim noticed the bands' blend of organic, tribal music left concertgoers in tears after the show. Fans expressed feeling transformed after hearing their music.

"We didn't really understand what we were doing at the time. We didn't understand any of the science of it. We just knew that it was working," Donovan described. After settling down and starting a family, Jim found himself teaching at Saint Francis University. He decided to use this opportunity to learn the science behind the reactions the audience had experienced when he had performed. He researched what was happening to the brain and body when someone drummed for an extended period of time.

What he found was that the brain goes through chemical changes when listening to music. "One is that we get this chemical called endorphins. These are natural painkillers or natural 'feel good' chemicals," Donovan said. "When we synchronize with the beat of music, our brains are literally in training with the pattern. That synchronization starts to develop a chemical called oxytocin, which is a bonding hormone."

Not only does listening to music increase the communication capabilities of the brain, but it also triggers the production of chemicals associated with happiness and connection—which explains a lot as to why we naturally gravitate to our favorite playlists. Over the years, we have created chemical connections in our brains that bring about natural increases in mood.

Music's Effect on the Body

Music also has the ability to help heal the body when it synchronizes our natural rhythms of breath and beat. Dr. David Lewis-Hodgson, Chairman and Founder of Mindlab International, conducted a study where participants were asked to solve challenging puzzles while listening to music.

The researchers measured brain activity, heart rate, blood pressure, and breathing rate. When the song "Weightless" by Marconi Union was playing, it reduced a person's overall anxiety level by 65 percent while also reducing their natural rhythms by 35 percent.

Marconi Union's song was created in collaboration with sound therapists to have "carefully arranged harmonies, rhythms, and bass lines that help slow a listener's heart rate, reduce blood pressure, and lower levels of the stress hormone cortisol," (Curtin, 2017). The song has been known to be effective enough to cause drowsiness and is advised not to be listened to while driving. It is capable of not only releasing stress-reducing chemical effects within the brain but also providing beneficial physical effects as well.

In her TED Talk, pianist Robin Spielberg describes how she went into pre-term labor at just twenty-two weeks into her pregnancy with twin baby girls. After being on bed rest in the hospital for eleven days, Robin had to have an emergency C-section performed due to an infection threatening the lives of both her and the babies. Sadly, only one baby girl survived, weighing only twelve ounces.

While her daughter received lifesaving support in the Neonatal Intensive Care Unit (NICU), Robin noticed how loud and busy the environment was—the opposite of what she expected was needed for healing. She desperately wanted to play her piano to drown out some of the noise. Robin decided to do the next best thing by bringing her own CD recordings and asking the nurses to play them for her daughter over the four months she spent there.

Nurses noticed that when the recordings were playing, her child's breathing, pulse, and oxygen levels would stabilize. Her daughter, Valerie, survived and thrived. As Valerie grew and developed, Robin was also able to correlate her learning abilities with music. She discovered during elementary school that when she sang the information Valerie needed to learn, the little girl was able to more easily retain it and even sing it back. This finding helped her go from a C to an A student.

Indre Viskontas, a neuroscientist and opera singer, was interviewed on PBS and further explained the physical effects of music on the body. "The parts of our brain that are engaged in beat processing are the same parts of our brain that are engaged in motor planning and motor actions. So, we actually feel it within our bodies." Like our heartbeat and respiratory rate, our biological rhythms are also stimulated and align themselves to the different beats or rhythms of songs; this stabilizes physical properties within our body, providing healing.

How to Incorporate Music into Your Healing

I remember the expression on my manager's face the first time I mentioned it was "time to put on my headphones, listen to Enya, and focus." It was a combination of shock mixed with a touch of curiosity. I needed to finish an analysis for an audit, and working in a large, open room with six other people made it difficult to concentrate.

He replied, "Enya, huh? I never pictured you as the type."

My husband had a similar reaction when he was first subjected to Andrew Belle on a car ride during our vacation in Washington. Now, three years later, anytime I am the one behind the wheel when we get in the car as a family, he selects the Andrew Belle radio on Pandora before I even have time to back out of our driveway.

Everyone has their own unique musical preferences. My manager can almost always be heard with jazz playing in his office, and my husband cleans the house with Mexican cumbia music blaring.

Whether you pick songs based on your current mood, time of day, or the activity you are participating in, the options are endless. No matter what your favorite artist or playlist is, the overall healing effects for your mind, body, and soul are proven to be beneficial. Incorporating music into your everyday life is a vital tool for your overall well-being. Where can you incorporate music into your daily life?

1. Create playlists

With millions of songs produced each year worldwide, your playlist options are endless. They can be created to help elevate or reduce your current mood or for specific activities in your day.

- Feeling anxious or stressed? Here's a recommended playlist from Melanie Curtin's article on Inc.com entitled "Neuroscience Says Listening to This Song Reduces Anxiety by Up to 65 Percent." The playlist is available to download on Spotify:

  1. "Weightless"—Marconi Union
  2. "Electra"—Airstream
  3. "Mellomaniac (Chill Out Mix)"—DJ Shah
  4. "Watermark"—Enya
  5. "Strawberry Swing"—Coldplay
  6. "Please Don't Go"—Barcelona
  7. "Pure Shores"—All Saints
  8. "Someone Like You"—Adele
  9. "Canzonetta Sull'aria"—Mozart
  10. "We Can Fly"—Rue du Soleil (Café Del Mar)

- Feeling sad or down? Here's a list of songs to help you cope with depression from Akanksha Soni's article for Calm Sage.

    1. "Three Little Birds"—Bob Marley
    2. "Alive"—Sia
    3. "1-800-273-8255"—Logic
    4. "I Won't Give Up"—Jason Mraz
    5. "Weightless"—Natasha Bedingfield
    6. "Scars to Your Beautiful"—Alessia Cara
    7. "Nothing Else Matters"—Metallica
    8. "Undefeated"—Daughtry
    9. "Swim"—Jack's Mannequin
    10. "Fight Song"—Rachel Platten

- Hate going grocery shopping and weaving around the endless sea of shopping carts as much as I do? Bring your headphones and put on your favorite pump-up playlist.
- Do you commute to work and find yourself battling road rage while sitting in traffic? Tune to your favorite radio station and sing your heart out in the car.

2. Make music yourself

- Did you learn to play an instrument as a child, or have you always wanted to learn how? Grab your favorite instrument and let your own music heal you. Even if you don't have one, use your hands to drum or clap to the beat of a song.

3. Dance it out

- Put on your favorite songs and let the beat of the music take over your body. It doesn't matter if you are in the shower, commuting to work, or cooking dinner; let loose and dance.
- Feeling angry or upset? Practice "rage dancing" by turning on some loud music and moving your body however it wants to move. By the end of the song, I guarantee you will feel a sense of release and calm.

CHAPTER 3

MY PILLARS OF SUPPORT

———

"Be strong enough to stand alone,
smart enough to know when you need help,
and brave enough to ask for it."

—ZIAD ABDELNOUR

After silently struggling with depression for most of his adult life, Jake Tyler found himself overwhelmed trying to remember what feeling happy was like or when the last time he had genuinely felt happy. Whenever anyone asked how he was doing, he always replied, "I'm fine."

Jake had come to lean on this response as a way to deflect others from uncovering what was really going on. He had gotten really good at convincing friends and family that he was *okay*. He did not yet understand the self-destruction that comes with not letting anybody in. When I listened to his TEDxBrighton talk titled "'I'm Fine'—Learning to Live With Depression," his definition of depression resonated with me. Jake stated, "Depression, the biggest, most all-inclusive club in the world, that convinces each person they are the only member" (Tyler, 2017).

Jake recalled the morning when the darkness seemed to overcome him, and he had come to the conclusion that taking his life was the only option. What he had intended to be his goodbye call to his mother became a beacon of light bright enough for Jake to agree to seek help.

The next day, one question from his doctor left him awestruck in its simpleness: "Do you actually want to die, or do you just not want to feel like this anymore?"

After receiving help from his doctor, Jake realized one day that he was getting better upon discovering he was twelve miles into taking his dog for a walk. He described the realization of the scenery around him suddenly looking "normal" again and the colors surrounding him exploding in their realness.

The fog of depression seemed to have evaporated, and with it, a sudden awareness of the beauty and good feelings one receives when in nature. A warming sensation filled his body, the corners of his lips curling upward. He concluded that walking and being out in nature, in combination with help from his doctor, was what had brought back his happiness.

Desperate to keep this new feeling from disappearing as quickly as it had emerged, Jake went straight into town to buy a map of Great Britain. He sat, frantically circling places in his country that would keep him longing to be outside. A line suddenly appeared, a route that connected all the dots. He felt that if he documented his journey, it could inspire others.

His trek ended up being a three thousand-mile odyssey that he called "Black Dog Walks."

Preparing and planning for his trip was easy—almost seemingly effortless. However, explaining the "*why*" behind it to friends and family meant exposing his deepest and darkest secrets. He describes it as "the worst thing I ever had to do and the best thing I ever did," (Tyler, 2017).

Jake was overwhelmed by the amount of support he received in response and how many others he discovered were going through the same experience. By the time he reached North Wales, he was getting messages from strangers all around the country. They wanted to share their experiences with depression—with this acting for most as the first time they could openly express them—because they felt only Jake would be able to understand how they were feeling.

Jake provided a form of connection for others in talking about his feelings of depression and was building a community. This development brought with it another realization: exposing one's depression meant leveling the playing field. "Deep down everyone craves human connection" and "in the face of depression, people can achieve big things," (Tyler, 2017).

Jake's epiphany intensified when he received an opportunity to join nine others, all tackling mental health issues, to train for a marathon and tell their story to the nation. Captured in the BBC documentary *Mind Over Marathon*, Jake describes the psychological and physical hardships of the last fifth of the marathon.

He felt as if he was suddenly running the race wearing a suit of armor, treading through a body of water. Managing to overcome complete exhaustion, he crossed the finish line— and realized that the physical feat was just the backdrop of the occasion. The community and connection he made with others along the way were the true rewards.

I connected with Jake's story on many levels. Similar to my own experience, being out in nature and walking helped Jake heal. He also found community through talking with others about his mental health struggles. Depression really does lead you to feel like you are standing alone on a deserted island with no one to reach out to rescue you. I can't stress enough the importance others' support plays in maintaining stability when managing your mental illness. I have been fortunate enough to have many people step in and surround me with love and light in my darkest of times.

My Second Moms

After withdrawing from Trinity University and returning home in 2004 feeling like a complete failure, I was in a dark, unstable place.

After being back home for a few weeks, my parents happened to take one of our cats to the veterinarian they had used since before I was born: Century Animal Hospital.

Growing up, both Doctors Nairn and Van Brunt let me put on a stethoscope and listen to my pet's heartbeat or use the otoscope to look in their ears during appointments. They even had a jar with an animal heart that was infected with heartworms. As a child, I was fascinated by it all and even aspired to be a veterinarian like them.

While my parents were at the appointment, Dr. Nairn asked them how I was doing. They explained that I had been struggling with my mental health and that they weren't quite sure what would happen next. Dr. Nairn graciously suggested to them that I come work at the clinic and spend time around animals. She had experience with her brother and his own battle with schizophrenia and felt like she could help.

My parents returned home and let me know about the opportunity Dr. Nairn had offered. I was hesitant at first; but, after talking with her over the phone, I started at Century a few weeks later. Initially, I tended to the animals in the kennel area and helped the technicians when they needed assistance holding animals for treatments. I was glad to have something that motivated me to get out of bed in the morning and being around the animals was undoubtedly therapeutic. My mood improved over the next few months, and I became stable enough to enroll at Texas State University the following semester.

After completing two semesters at Texas State, I was feeling "normal" again and believed that I had gained back control of my mental illness. Seeing as I had established prolonged mental stability, Dr. Hauser offered to switch me to a new mood stabilizer because Lamictal made me overly drowsy. After several weeks on the new prescription, I was feeling elated and full of energy. I convinced myself that I didn't need to take medication anyone, thinking *it must have all been a phase of my adolescence.*

I also decided at that time that I needed a different job more tailored to college life. I quit my job at Century and took a position at a retail store in the outlet mall near the university. It didn't take long during training to realize this new job wasn't my thing, and on my first official day, I called in to quit. Of course, now I know that it was the mania controlling my thinking.

With my tail tucked and my mania on its way back down, I decided to go back to Century to see if I could do more of the front office work since I was switching my major to accounting. Dr. Nairn, ever helpful, agreed.

Without medication, the pendulum swung back towards depression, and I found myself sitting in the enclosed front office area at work, crying for good portions of the day. Nancy, a loyal, long-term employee at Century, and Dr. Nairn took me under their wing and took turns sitting and talking with me. I finally confessed I had stopped taking my medication, and they encouraged me to let my parents and psychiatrist know.

Looking back, my coworkers at Century supported me whenever I needed it, whether they understood what was happening or not. Nancy and Dr. Nairn were especially accommodating, and I could have never received that level of love and support at any other job. I am eternally grateful for them.

After graduating college and starting my career in accounting, I couldn't tolerate being away from Century. Dr. Nairn allowed me to come in the early mornings to do the bookkeeping, which continued until she sold the practice and retired. We still all keep in touch through phone calls, group texts, and small gatherings. It is a bond that will last a lifetime.

My Inner Circle

Of course, I have to credit my mother for being the rock in my support system; even though she didn't initially understand what was happening or why—she kept trying and trying until she found someone and something to help me. Now that I am older and a parent myself, I can't imagine the strength it took her to see her child suffer as much as I did and to fear the worst that could happen. She must have felt so helpless during the early years. Regardless of the situation I was in, she always told me, "I love you no matter what." She's become my sounding board for any obstacle with which I'm struggling.

Then there's my husband, Tony, who has stuck by me for fifteen years and knows the exact kind of support I require at any given time. When I'm feeling down, a single hug from him provides me with the comfort I need. He's my best friend, and I can genuinely express any thoughts or feelings in a safe space with him. We started dating after high school and have matured and grown together. He has mastered the art of reading my emotions. He calls me on my bluffs and knows when I just need a little tough love to push me forward.

One night, I explained my frustrations with work and how I felt trapped in the financial comfort of my corporate accounting job; in response, he suggested I start looking for a new job or start my entrepreneurial journey with coaching. At the time, I didn't think I had enough street cred to start a coaching practice.

I went on to make a few more financial-based excuses when he looked at me and said, "Kate, you don't give yourself any credit. You are determined. You were able to stop all your medications so that we could start a family, and you have been able to stay off of them for years! I think you have forgotten that."

I skipped a breath. Tony had hit the nail on the head, and it caught me off-guard. Now, anytime I begin to feel my self-confidence dip, I reflect back on his comments and then start listing the things I have accomplished in my life and remind myself of my successes.

My relationship with my sister, Natalie, has been one of transformation. We were adopted four years apart and had different biological parents. Growing up, we fought often and had polar opposite tastes and personalities. I love sports and being athletic; she loves being artistic and creative. Come to think of it, I think she would be content to go her whole life without ever sweating on purpose.

The "oil and water" dynamic of our relationship lasted into early adulthood. It wasn't until right before I became pregnant with Alice that we started talking regularly. She was the first person I shared my positive pregnancy test result with—besides Tony, of course. I shared with her my joys and experiences of being pregnant for the first time, and she was thrilled to become an aunt. At the same time, she was going through a strained marriage and needed someone with whom to talk. Our sisterly bond strengthened even further after she was in a horrible car accident that left her needing a spinal fusion and facing a long road to recovery.

She is now happily remarried and a successful pastry chef for an upscale catering company in Austin. Her back has healed successfully. We talk weekly, and she is now one of my biggest sounding boards. I know she will forever be a member of my inner-circle support system, and I couldn't imagine not having her as my sister and confidante.

My daughter has become my greatest source of strength. One look at her, and I can weather any storm. It doesn't matter how sad or upset I am; when she walks in the room, I instantly transform into Super Woman because I strive to be my best self whenever she's near me. Children walk around with so much joy and wonder for this world; I don't want to take any of that from her. Her happiness is contagious, and all she has is love to give.

Going through coaching certification has given me access to many amazing people who are full of fantastic, positive energy and have allowed me an additional level of support to reach out to whenever I need it. I have never found such a large group of people who are always willing to support and uplift their colleagues. I made friendships in my training modules that will last a lifetime. The community that iPEC has created truly lives to raise the consciousness level of anyone around them. I am elevated every day when I read others' posts or inspirational messages in their online communities.

Ask for Help

The strength of my current support system acts as a vital pillar of my mental stability. It is the biggest contributing factor to my current ability to manage my mind during periods of depression and anxiety. My spiritual journey has given me the skills to know that I can shift my mood by simply having a phone call with someone in my support system. This opportunity allows me to process my feelings verbally with someone I trust with my whole heart to choose how I want to feel moving forward. To know I have others who will support me through the good times and the bad means I will never be on my mental health journey alone.

It's taken me quite a while to be comfortable opening up and telling people how I feel or the thoughts I'm having. I am introverted by nature. Nowadays, I have no problem sharing my feelings or thoughts with others whom I trust. I've learned, people can help.

The worst thing you can do when suffering from a mental illness is to keep it all inside. You have to share it with someone no matter how much you want to keep it to yourself. It is okay to lean on others when you feel like you don't have the strength to carry on. It is ALWAYS okay to ask for help. All you need is for *just one person* to hear you in that moment and partner with you to get help. You don't have to be in it all alone—that's just the disease talking.

As humans, we all crave connection and belonging; but, the disease, combined with the added stigma around mental health, leaves those who struggle feeling isolated. Support systems can be made up of family members, friends, coworkers, peer groups, and other community members. They can provide the connection and support you need.

Technology has granted us the ability to pick up our phones and instantly connect with anyone worldwide. Take advantage of these times. If COVID-19 has taught us anything, it's how much we truly need social connection with people we care about.

CHAPTER 4

THE SHIFT

———

"Nothing is impossible. The word itself
says 'I'm possible.'"

—AUDREY HEPBURN

You don't have to suffer the rest of your life with bipolar disorder. But, it does mean that you're going to have to practice and strengthen mindset techniques to help manage the ups and downs that come with it.

Since I've accomplished long-term stability in my mental health journey, people around me may take for granted how much effort I put into maintaining my stability and well-being on a daily basis. I didn't just wake up one day and suddenly stop having the disorder affect me.

I've had to learn and study myself at a deep level. My understanding of my own awareness, combined with practices that take care of my body and tap into my spiritual connection, complete my stability package.

Two of the most crucial mindset methods I have learned on my journey are self-reflection and self-awareness. I was finally able to gain control of my illness when I decided that *enough was enough*. After going through several periods of deep depression and the darkest part of my illness with my attempted suicide, the light became stronger and clearer. I made a promise to myself never to return to that dark and destructive place again.

Has it been easy? *No.* There are low moments and months that might be filled with anxiety.

The key to my shift in how bipolar disorder affects me was my realization that it does not define me. I no longer chose to give it the power to control my life. I realized that the disease affects my brain—an organ—but I still have hold of the reigns over my mind and thoughts. There was a sudden awareness of a separation between the two.

That awareness came when I learned the practice of mindfulness.

Self-Reflection & Awareness

The power of your mindset can be truly remarkable and is the key to finding long-term stability with your mental health. For me, step one was learning to understand and listen to how my mind worked. Being able to be in control of your thoughts is not an easy task. It's a lot easier to live your life on autopilot by letting your brain roam in a never-ending cycle, thought after thought. You have to be able to stop and reflect on your recent actions or mood and believe that you have the power to change it.

In order to change your mood at any given moment, you have to find the thought that's causing you to feel the way you do. Then you can decide whether you want to change it. When you are able to identify the thought that is triggering the low level of emotion and change it to a more beneficial one, it becomes easier to take actions that help stabilize your mood. That is how I went from coping with my mental health to thriving with it.

The most accessible tool that I have found to do this is through mindfulness, the practice of being in the present and learning to observe one's thoughts and emotions from a distance, without any self-judgment. I first heard about mindfulness from my psychiatrist, Dr. Hauser. She had suggested it in my session after my panic attack while driving to work.

Dr. Hauser believes in mindfulness meditation so much that she founded MBCT Austin, a mindfulness-based cognitive therapy course. In her talk, *The Effects of Mindfulness Meditations on Medical Conditions*, she discusses a study conducted by Britta K. Hölzel, a German neuroscientist and researcher, in 2010 that evaluated MRI scans of individuals before and after participating in an eight-week program of Mindfulness-Based Stress Reduction.

"Whole-brain analyses identified increases in the posterior cingulate cortex, the temporoparietal junction, and the cerebellum in the MBSR group compared to the controls. The results suggest that participation in MBSR is associated with changes in gray matter concentration in brain regions involved in learning and memory processes, emotion regulation, self-referential processing, and perspective-taking."

Dr. Hauser summarizes, "You can see over time, these stressed and otherwise healthy individuals developed an increase in their right-sided amygdala volume. At the same time, the MRI scan showed changes in the hippocampus."

In the online article "From Structure to Behavior in Basolateral Amygdala-Hippocampus Circuits," authors Ying Yang and Jian-Zhi Wang state, "The amygdala is specialized for input and processing of emotion, while the hippocampus is essential for declarative or episodic memory. During emotional reactions, these two brain regions interact to translate the emotion into particular outcomes."

In other words, these two parts of the brain are responsible for processing experienced life events and deciding what type of emotion is triggered. Mindfulness practices directly contribute to growth in this area of the brain, allowing a person to better regulate emotions and reactions to outside stressors. This newfound ability is a vital tool for those of us who struggle with mood disorders.

I first started mindfulness training using meditation, first by focusing on my breath and then observing my current feelings. Meditation is a skill that takes practice. In the beginning, my head became flooded with constant invasive thoughts; but, as they came, I simply acknowledged them and then focused back on my breathing.

Over time, my intrusive thoughts decreased through my practice. I recommend starting with just five minutes and working up to twenty to thirty minutes every day. This time allows me to be an observer of my mind and body. With time came the clarity to observe my feelings without judgment and decide whether or not to change them.

I learned to continue the practice of mindfulness by incorporating it into my daily walks and runs. I make sure to focus on my surroundings and look up to the sky to notice how the clouds are formed that day. I feel the wind as it blows across my face, and then I check in with my muscles to sense any tension or discomfort in them. I observe the rhythm of my breath. This practice helps me to stay grounded and observe my mind and body.

At some point during every day, I ensure that I stop, check in with myself mentally, and ask, *"How am I doing? Do I need to seek help?"* It is a daily status check to see if an internal adjustment is needed. It may also mean I need to reach out to my inner support circle for a talk or guidance.

If an adjustment is needed, I come up with a plan for the day. I decide whether or not I need to focus on my mind, body, or spirit. Possibly, rest needs to be incorporated into my day by spending a few moments in my hammock swing. By simply reflecting on my current mental state, I can tweak my daily happiness plan to ensure my mental stability for that day.

In the beginning, it took months to recognize and acknowledge when my mood was negatively affecting me. But now, I can catch it within a few days, sometimes within a few hours. It's taken time and practice through self-reflection and awareness that comes with mindful meditation.

Making the Shift

Why is this good news? Anyone can learn to shift their mindset and observe their emotions from a distance. It just takes practice.

Start by learning to meditate. There are many applications available to download on your phone that are guided and designed to teach the practice—my personal go-to is Insight Timer. It allows users to choose between either a guided meditation or a timed meditation with ambient music or sounds, alongside offering multiple courses and talks that further cognizance toward the practice.

During meditation, you will begin to notice the types of thoughts that frequently pop into your mind. Don't judge yourself for what they are or how often they come. Just catch yourself in the thought, let it go gracefully, and refocus on the meditation. You will begin to notice the feeling of separation between your thoughts and your mind. With continued practice, your thoughts will become less frequent, and the space between them shall grow.

With this newfound understanding, you will be able to apply the same technique throughout your day. When you become aware of a current emotion that is keeping your mood low, you can then reflect on the *why* of that emotion. Once the underlying thought is identified, you can reframe it to be more positive or opportunistic.

Another technique is to choose the emotion you wish to feel and think of a time in your life that you remember feeling that way. Visualize your surroundings at that previous point in time. *Where were you? What were the sounds you were hearing? Who were you with?*

Paint the scene, then close your eyes, put yourself back in that time and remember what it felt like. You will notice your energy begin to shift, and you will start to feel that emotion again. Open your eyes whenever you are ready and return to the present moment—bringing your new energy and emotion along with you.

You don't have to believe every thought you have. Our brains are biologically designed to keep us safe and content with the status quo; it desires as little change as possible. When you try to move forward to new opportunities or make a change, the brain will try to talk you out of it. Since the future outcome is unknown, it seeks to protect you. While this instinct helps prevent us from ending up in unsafe situations, it does not assist in our efforts to grow and find stability with our mental health.

I've always been determined, and have never let anyone or my brain, tell me what I can and can't do. Some have described me as stubborn! I refused to accept that bipolar disorder would control my life. I believe that's the most important mindset a person with a mental illness has to have. You can make a promise to yourself that you won't let it control your life.

When you battle your way out of the darkness and have a glimpse back into a balanced life with stability, that is your moment. That's when you are at your best and able to find your inner strength. You are always stronger than you think. This disease can be a battle for your life. You need to suit up and do what it takes so that you can live a happy and stable life. *It is possible.*

YOU REALLY ARE WHAT YOU EAT

"Our food should be our medicine and
our medicine should be our food."

—HIPPOCRATES

I weighed more than I ever had before, and I was eating as if I was sixteen years old and still playing basketball every day. One morning, a conversation with a coworker about New Year's resolutions inspired us to start a ninety-day weight loss challenge at work for the coming new year.

Thinking about my strategy for the challenge on my lunch break that day, I pondered what diet to try. Then I remembered the documentary *Forks over Knives*, where Doctors Campbell and Esselstyn advocate for a plant-based, whole-food diet to reduce heart and other chronic diseases.

My father had been on a similar but stricter cardiovascular-focused diet to prevent re-accumulation of plaque in his carotid arteries after life-saving surgery. It had resulted in a ninety-pound weight loss and clear arterial scans for more than ten years now.

Upon agreeing to the challenge with my coworkers, I went home that evening and re-watched *Forks over Knives*. I was shocked, after hearing again, how much food production of animals plays a primary role in climate change in our world today. The alarming situation the meat and dairy industry has created in America inspired me not to just start a diet but to change my lifestyle for the environment, knowing weight loss would follow.

The sudden change in my diet brought many challenges. I had always been a picky eater when it came to fruits and vegetables but had heard that my palette would adjust over time. Some people say it takes over fifteen times of trying a food you don't like before your taste buds actually adapt to the food. On top of that, most of the food I currently had in my refrigerator and pantry was highly processed.

I also had to factor into account my husband's desire to continue eating animal products. I had initially shared the knowledge from the documentary with him, but he wasn't sold on the idea yet. I started preparing plant-based, whole food meals for dinner only to have him pick at it and then leave to go buy something from a local fast-food chain.

Obviously, this completely defeated the purpose, so I switched tactics by cooking an animal protein to complement the meal for him. That tactic was successful, and we settled into a routine. Seven years later, I still prepare meals throughout the week that alternate between predominately plant-based and comfort foods like pizza and hamburgers for him.

Going to the grocery store ended up taking twice as long. As we mainly were buying produce, I had to weigh and print the labels for each item. I paused in aisles to review all the ingredients on any essential packaged foods while resisting the urge to pick up typical items I was used to grabbing. Cooking food from scratch meant more time in the kitchen and the need to have more spices and basic ingredients on hand. It was frustrating to adjust to the increase in time to prepare and build new habits, but I was motivated to make the change. I knew losing weight would make me feel better physically, so I used that motivation to fight through my frustrations.

The first week of the challenge was certainly the hardest. The detox from caffeine and processed foods made my body sluggish and led to an almost constant dull headache. The reward for the first week, however, was nine pounds in lost weight.

As the weeks went by, the new rhythm of my lifestyle change fell into place. I felt better and better every day, and my energy levels rose dramatically. I didn't have to snack anymore since the food I was eating for my meals kept me full for hours at a time. The amount of weight loss each week got smaller, but the physical changes I could see in my body increased. I couldn't keep my pants up without the help of a belt, and my shirts seemed to drown my torso.

I felt terrific mentally, and my self-confidence was blossoming. According to Dr. Eva Selhub, in the Harvard Health blog article "Nutritional psychiatry: Your brain on food," 95 percent of our body's serotonin is produced in the gastrointestinal tract. The neurotransmitter serotonin, also known as nature's anti-depressant, "helps regulate sleep and appetite, mediate moods, and inhibit pain."

The imbalance of serotonin plays a significant role in bipolar disorder. By eating more quality foods in their whole,

unprocessed state, I was not only getting the physical benefits but mental ones, too. I believe my diet was changing my
body's chemistry and bringing more balance to the chemical
makeup in my brain, stabilizing my mood.

I ended up winning that office challenge, losing thir-
ty-nine pounds in ninety days. I not only won the $500 pool,
but I also felt physically better than I had in an exceedingly
long time. The change had also boosted my morale and provided a new sense of mental clarity. An added bonus was
that my lifestyle change also benefited others because I was
reducing my environmental footprint.

Nutrition's Healing Effects on the Mind

From the Institute for Optimum Nutrition's article, *Mood
Food: How nutrition affects your mental health*, having var-
ied bacteria in the gut, known as probiotics, is a positive
contributing factor to one's mental health. The gut not only
produces serotonin but also produces the natural "happy"
chemical, dopamine.

"Scientists call these psychobiotics—probiotics that can be
used to positively impact mental health by altering the way
the gut communicates with the brain. It's thought that in
depression, certain messages don't get through from the gut
to the brain" (Optimum Nutrition 2020). These types of beneficial probiotic bacteria can be found in foods that have been
fermented, such as yogurt, tempeh, kimchi, and kombucha.

I love getting kimchi in my tofu salad bowl when I grab
lunch at Chi'lantro, a local Korean BBQ-inspired restaurant
in Austin. The unique taste compliments the flavors of the
fresh greens and veggies. The growing trend of kombucha

means that I can grab the occasional bottle at my local grocery store and even at some gas stations now.

In his TEDx talk, "Food for Thought: How your belly controls your brain," biologist Ruairi Robertson explains that ninety percent of the cells in our body are actually bacterial cells that are as diverse as the Amazon rainforest. These bacterial cells play a vital role in communication between our brain and our belly—through the vagus nerve (Robertson, 2015).

Having the right combination of microbes in our gut is essential to both our physical and mental health. You can improve your gut health by including more dietary sources of prebiotics that help stimulate the growth of "good" bacteria. Some examples of common prebiotics include bananas, whole grains, beans, nuts, honey, and apples.

I love to combine pre- and probiotics in my morning snacks, like plant-based vanilla yogurt with crushed almonds, sliced banana, and a dribble of honey. Another go-to snack is sliced apple with almond butter.

In the article, "Nutritional psychiatry: Your brain on food," Dr. Eva Selhub, former director of the Benson Henry Institute for Mind-Body Medicine at Massachusetts General Hospital, states "studies have compared traditional diets, like the Mediterranean diet and the traditional Japanese diet, to a typical Western diet and have shown that the risk of depression is 25 percent to 35 percent lower in those who eat a traditional diet." This reduction is believed to be due to these diets being primarily made up of fruits, vegetables, seafood, and whole grains. They also are limited in lean meats and dairy. Since serotonin is the primary neurotransmitter for stabilizing mood, it makes sense that the more nutrition your diet contains, the better and more stable your mood is.

Some days I am guilty of consuming more processed foods than I like to admit, but I almost always start my day with a smoothie from my Nutribullet. It is an easy way to get my daily dose of fruits and leafy greens. I use the same recipe each time, starting with filling the bottom third of the cup with spinach, adding a banana, a scoop of Vegan chocolate protein powder, some frozen pineapple, then topping it off with a blend of frozen berries. I fill the cup with water, and after a few moments in the blender, breakfast is served. Freshly blended, it is a dark magenta color that turns browner with time. I take my time drinking it in the mornings, and it is very filling.

Occasionally at the office, I was frequently asked by my coworkers, "What exactly are you drinking?"

I always laughed and said, "It's a smoothie! But it tastes better than it looks, I promise!"

When I started working from home during the pandemic, my husband jumped on the smoothie train. He used to skip breakfast and rarely had time for lunch most days. He would come home from work "hangry" and lightheaded. One morning, he asked if I would make him a smoothie, too, and now, he will not leave for work until I have made him one.

Our gut is the second brain we never knew we had! Help improve the connection between your brain and your gut by eating foods that diversify and bring balance to your gut health.

How to Optimize Your Diet for Healing

You truly are what you eat! This perspective doesn't mean that you can never enjoy a sugary treat like a brownie or cupcake again or can't indulge in your favorite greasy hamburger and french fries from time to time. It just means that those "treats" need to be a small percentage of your weekly diet. It may be difficult to first track how much and what types of foods you should be eating every day. I found Dr. Greger's Daily Dozen app to be a helpful tool in ensuring I hit my daily nutritional needs with its simple checklist format.

"Traditionalize" your diet by eating more fruits, vegetables, and whole grains while limiting your consumption of animal products. Remember that a little goes a long way! You don't have to make the drastic change overnight as I did. Start with eating plant-based, whole foods one meal a day and work your way to more. The effects will bring positive benefits to your mental and physical health while reducing your carbon footprint. That sounds like a win-win to me!

Going plant-based doesn't mean you can never eat meat again. Even reducing your animal product consumption to a few times a week has a significant impact. I choose to eat meat only once or twice a year when we go to our BBQ anniversary dinner at the Salt Lick. We had it catered for our wedding and decided to start a tradition of eating there annually on our anniversary. I also partake in the annual auditor-provided lunch from Franklins BBQ. What can I say? I am a Texas girl!

I have been committed to this lifestyle change ever since that first weight loss challenge. Somedays, I am stricter about following it than others. However, I have noticed that in those periods when my diet is composed of more processed foods, my mood suffers. In periods of stress, I reach for the fast, convenient option of processed foods, which has an almost immediate negative effect on my body and mind.

I don't think it's a coincidence that my diet change coincided with the stability I had attained in the last five years on my mental health journey. I think it actually was the spark that first allowed me to be more open-minded about different ways of living. Simply put—the cleaner I eat, the better my mood.

CHAPTER 6

THE MARATHON

—

"Exercise is the key not only to physical health
but to peace of mind."

—NELSON MANDELA

When I was a child, my parents purchased over one hundred
acres in the Texas Hill Country across the highway from our
neighborhood. Every time we would go out to the property,
my dad would have me get out and open the gate, and I would
take off running while my parents followed me in the truck.

Slowly but surely, I made my way for miles around the property. Eventually, I'd get tired and join them back in the truck.
It was something I did almost every time we went out there.

In middle school, I joined the track team. I loved participating in the high jump, hurdles, and relays but longed for
the opportunity to compete in high school cross country. I
looked forward to the long-distance running that I enjoyed
so much as a child.

In high school, one of the best things about those morning training runs for cross country was being up and awake while accomplishing something so early in the morning. There was a slight tinge of coldness in the air and darkness that began to break into the light of the sunrise. I mostly just loved the solidarity that comes with running as a group, but also by myself.

After high school, I got away from running. But in my adult years, when the pounds started to pack on, my first inclination was always to return to running. One of those times of trying to get back into motion, I started to go on walks with my manager on the trail around Lady Bird Lake in Austin.

We started fast-paced walking, averaging thirteen-minute miles. It was the perfect combination of exercise and nature, alongside being something that we could easily do right after work. After a couple of months of this routine, one morning, I found a printout of information about running the 3M Half Marathon in Austin on my desk. I immediately knew who the culprit was. After scanning the document, I decided I was going to train for my first half marathon. I had never run 13.1 miles—but knew I needed good running shoes and a training plan.

The hot Texas summer was finally giving way to cooler weather on that October day in 2015. I headed to the REI store down the street on my lunch break. A store associate helped me find the perfect pair of Brooks running shoes that would support my previously injured knee.

I switched my focus to finding a training plan. After googling for the rest of my lunch break, I decided on a highly rated app that eased the user into running, with incremental intervals of walking.

The app's training plan was twelve weeks long and included running four days a week, one to two days of non-impact cardio, and a couple of rest days. Lunch breaks became my time for training during the workweek. I could hit the trail about an hour before everyone's usual lunchtime and enjoy the solitude of the trail before it got busy.

After training for a month, I began to look forward to my time alone, running in nature while listening to music and playing the mental game that comes with running long-distance. I also loved running on the gravel path of the trail. It's less of an impact on joints than the concrete of a sidewalk or asphalt of a road. It took me back to my days of running cross country races.

A week before the race, I found out that my manager and the other people I thought would be joining me for the run had suddenly decided that they weren't conditioned enough to participate.

I was going to be doing this race *alone.*

My heart sank after finding out I'd be running by myself. However, I found comfort in the fact that I had put in the training required to finish the race. I focused on drawing momentum and inspiration from the cheering crowds on race day instead of from my peers as participants. I knew my mother would be waiting for me at various spots throughout the race and ended up spending the night before the race at my parents' house. My brother was going to join us to cheer me on as well.

The morning of the race, my mom, brother, and I woke up and headed out for the long drive to North Austin. As we neared the parking garage from the opposite side of the highway, I could see the long line of cars going down the access road. We exited and did a U-turn to get our place in the line.

The line of cars just crept towards the parking garage, the minutes ticked by faster and faster. I suddenly found myself with less than twenty minutes to go before the race started, and we were not even in the parking garage. I had a whole plan for my warmup routine and how to work out the nerves before the race. There wasn't going to be time for that.

We were able to finally make it to the parking garage, park the car, and the three of us raced down the stairs to the start line. I was incredibly worried that I wouldn't be able to warm up my muscles in time and would end up pulling something at the start of the race.

That morning, the temperature was just below freezing. I frantically ran in place, jumped up and down, stretched dynamically, and kept my clothing layers on until the very last moment.

The announcer counted down to the start of the race. I stripped down to my base layer but decided to keep the added warmth of my gloves and sweatband. I hate the feeling that comes with numb ears and fingers in the cold. The runners in each time group started moving forward towards the start line.

I finally crossed the start, racing to the outside line of my group to get some much-needed space to find my stride. No sooner had I finally gotten into position when I looked up in time to see a woman holding a sign. "0.1 miles down, 13 to go."

Talk about a buzzkill.

The chill of the air felt like I had icicles inside my lungs. Layers of other runners' clothing became obstacles in the road. Finally, as I felt the buzz of the first-mile marker on my watch, I had good positioning within the group. It was just in time to go over the bridge and see the sun piercing the skyline.

I was running at a phenomenal pace. My first six miles were faster than I had run during my training. I made sure to stop at every water station and felt confident about the next seven miles. The first part of the run was primarily flat, with a few stretches of downhills. The second half of the race proved more difficult.

There were several stretches of hill running, and about mile eight, going into mile nine, I hit my first "wall" running up one of the largest hills I had encountered thus far.

How am I running this?

Why am I running this?

Oh my gosh, I just want to stop and walk the rest of the way.

I knew if I stopped running, I would succumb to my desire to walk and that I might not be able to convince myself to start running again. So, I did not stop.

I continued to fight through the temptation of walking as I approached the top of the hill. There were several spectators with signs cheering the runners. It gave me the energy boost I desperately needed to continue running. I pushed through mile nine and was approaching mile ten when I saw my mom and brother positioned to cheer me on. It brought a new wave of emotional energy and the will to continue that saved me at that point.

I continued through mile eleven, but as I ran mile twelve, I felt my body become a heavy, sluggish weight. My legs felt weighted more and more with each stride.

Just in time, there was another long stretch of spectators. This time, there were several children all reaching out to get high fives from the racers. I made sure to run and high-five every single one of them.

At mile thirteen, I began to realize *I could actually do this.* But as my strides continued, what was supposed to be a mile seemed like three. Each step felt heavier and heavier, and my desire to walk was stronger than ever. That impulse was compounded by the fact that there appeared to be very few spectators in this final mile. For some reason, there weren't a lot of other race participants around me, either. This stretch was going to be the final mental battle, or so I thought. Suddenly I remembered the power of having a mantra. I found myself repeating in my head: *I can do this. I can do this. I can do this.*

I started to see the spectators again, and I could hear the announcer at the finish line. Hope was near. I turned the corner to see the most massive hill of the entire race. *Who does this? Who designed a race with the last tenth of it introducing its most brutal obstacle?*

My mantra turned into, *One more step, one more step, one more step.* As my legs began to burn more than I had ever experienced, it felt like I was running through fire. By the time I made it to the top of the hill, there was a hard left turn. I could see the finish line and the masses of people. I wanted to finish strong. I told myself, *Okay, this is it. Let's do it. Give it everything you've got.*

It felt like I was running fast, but then I started to notice others race right by me. I finally crossed the finish line and was corralled by other runners, exhausted but accomplished. Before I could even catch my breath, I was given my "finisher" medal, handed a bag of food, water, and a banana. As the corral of runners was pushed through, I caught a glimpse of my mom and brother waiting for me.

I'd done it.

I'd run my first half marathon. The four months of training had paid off.

Exercising Towards a Goal

Psychotherapist, Dr. Sarah Gingell, in an article for *Psychology Today* entitled "How Your Mental Health Reaps the Benefits of Exercise," shares, "It is now clear that exercise reduces the likelihood of depression and also maintains our mental health as we age.

On the treatment side, exercise appears to be as good as existing pharmacological interventions across a range of conditions, such as mild to moderate depression, dementia, and anxiety, and even reduces cognitive issues in schizophrenia." Daily exercise is yet another method to help boost your mood while also benefitting your body.

Dr. Gingell's article also shares that "Psychiatrist Madhukar Trivedi has shown that three or more sessions per week of aerobic exercise or resistance training, for 45 to 60 minutes per session, can help treat even chronic depression. Effects tend to be noticed after about four weeks, and training should be continued for 10-12 weeks for the greatest antidepressant effect."

Training for a race isn't the only way to reap the benefits of exercise. Aerobic exercise can include biking, swimming, dancing, gardening, climbing stairs, or even mowing the lawn. If going for a run seems daunting, stay home, put on some music, and dance. You just need to move your body and get your heart rate up.

I continued to go through phases of running, participating in my second half marathon in early 2020. I have begun training for a full marathon in 2022. It can be hard on the body, but having a race to train for, gives me the motivation I need to continue. Between races and when I am healing from injuries, I also enjoy just walking. Dedicating thirty minutes daily to moving my body is another must in my personal happiness recipe. It satisfies the body corner of my stability triangle but can also benefit the mind and spirit as well.

Sometimes on my walks or runs, I listen to music. Other days, I listen to a self-help or spiritual audiobook. There are times I leave my AirPods at home and practice mindfulness by listening to the sounds around me, feeling the breeze brush my skin, or tuning into different muscles in my body and how they feel.

I also practice yoga. As with walking or running, I am able to satisfy the body, mind, and spirit components at the same time. My daughter has taken a liking to yoga. She has claimed my mat as hers and frequently requests "kids yoga" on the TV so she can have her exercise time. She has even mastered several poses, and I am envious of her natural flexibility.

In this modern age, I think too many of us have lost the physical movement we as humans need. I know how hard it is to even get out of bed when your mood is low, but even a short walk can trigger the endorphin release in your brain. That release can be enough to get you through the next moment or even to complete a task you've been putting off.

We've all heard the saying "a body in motion stays in motion," and I enjoy movement and the accomplishment of daily physical activity. Some days, it's just a short walk around the block with my daughter, and that's okay. I just make sure I keep moving. What exercise goal can you set? How would it feel when you accomplish that goal? Growth comes with action, so set your goal and get your body moving.

CHAPTER 7

GET SOME REST

"Sleep is that golden chain that ties
health and our bodies together."

—THOMAS DEKKER

At night, I can lay my head down on my pillow and be asleep the next second. It drives my husband crazy! It can take him hours to fall asleep at night, but sleep comes easily for me.

I try to get at least seven hours of sleep every night. Anything less than that, and I feel it the next day, not only physically but mentally. I become tired and easily agitated, and everything seems to take more effort, including maintaining a positive mood and mindset.

Dr. Hauser told me sleep was the most important factor when it came time to having a child and maintaining my mental stability. This is especially true in the early months after giving birth, when parents go months without a full, uninterrupted night's sleep. It would be vital to maintaining my mood, and she was absolutely right.

In an article titled "Interventions for Sleep Disturbance in Bipolar Disorder," on the NCBI's website, it is stated that "experimental studies suggest that sleep deprivation can trigger a manic relapse. There is evidence that sleep deprivation can have an adverse impact on emotion regulation the following day."

The stresses of parenthood are completely unknown before actually becoming a parent. Sleep deprivation can be one of the hardest parts of parenthood. I was fortunate that Tony was present at that appointment with Dr. Hauser and understood how important sleep would be for me. Even though I still had to wake up and pump breast milk in the middle of the night to maintain my supply, he bore the brunt of the first six months of Alice's life on the night shift.

I've always been a heavy sleeper, and with the added burdens of parenthood, it intensified. Tony is a light sleeper who can get by on just a few hours of sleep at night. Now that Alice is older, he still is almost always the first to wake up if she so much as turns over in bed across the house.

Climbing the ladder in corporate America while being a wife and a mother meant that getting a full night's sleep and critical rest was something I rarely experienced. It was a lesson I learned the hard way.

One weekend when Alice was two years old, Tony had left on a guy's trip. He had always been good about taking time out to relax, hang out with friends, and enjoy life. I was more focused on spending my free time worrying about my work and my newfound duties as a mother. Alice and I hung out at the house, having a "chill" girls' weekend. I had never slept well when Tony was away, so I spent most of the weekend catching up on doing laundry, washing dishes, and cleaning instead of resting and relaxing.

That following Monday morning, I woke up with a knot in my right shoulder close to my neck, something I had never experienced before. The pain was excruciating, spreading throughout my right shoulder and up my neck. It was so intense that I could barely move. Somehow, I managed to get up from the bed and staggered towards the bathroom. The next thing I knew, I was lying face down on the cold, hard concrete floor of my master bathroom.

My head hurt. Pain was coming from the top right side of my forehead. I attempted to raise my head off the floor and, for what seemed like minutes, tried to remember anything. Finally, a thought came. *Why am I on the bathroom floor?*

I could hear Alice crying through the baby monitor in her bedroom. I wondered, *Why hasn't Tony gone to get her? Doesn't he know I'm lying on the floor?* Consciousness slowly began to return. *Tony's not here. It's just me.* Alice must have woken me back up. I had to go get her. *How long had I been unconscious?*

I somehow managed to push myself off the floor and stood somewhat upright. My gaze caught my image in the mirror, and there was a knot on the right side of my forehead.

The floor seemed to be rocking, so I kept one hand on the wall as I stumbled to Alice's bedroom. I bent over to lift her from the crib and suddenly felt the return of the excruciating pain in my neck and shoulder. Somehow, I managed to lift her with just my left arm, carefully and slowly. *What now?*

My skin was clammy. The pain was intensifying. I was fearful I would faint again, this time with her in my arms. I stumbled down the hall, leaning against the wall in case I got lightheaded. Finally, I made it to the couch and sat down, staring blankly into the living room.

My body shook as the intensity of the pain increased. My head hurt. *Oh yeah. I have a knot on my head.* I was dazed, and I knew my thoughts weren't clear. With Tony out of town, I had to call my parents. Somehow, my cell phone happened to be in the pocket of my jammies.

I dialed my mom. It was early, about 6:30 a.m., so I knew she would still be asleep and likely startled from my call.

As the phone was ringing, I started feeling lightheaded again and felt like I might pass out. As soon as I felt myself going limp, she answered. I snapped out of it, long enough to tell her that I had fallen and hit my head and that I didn't know what was really going on, but I needed help.

Her medical training must have kicked in. She asked me a series of questions. She then asked if Alice was okay. I told her that I would just sit there with her on the couch until she could get there. Calling an ambulance had been discussed.

I waited 45 minutes as my mom quickly dressed and drove from Dripping Springs to my house in San Marcos. Once she got there, I immediately felt relieved. Thankfully, I had been able to stay conscious the entire time.

All I could think about was that I needed to get ready to go to work. *I was fine; it wasn't a big deal.* But with her medical background, she insisted I go get checked out.

After an internet search, I found a minor emergency clinic that was already open. I called, and they said they could see me right away. Once there, they did several tests and said that it seemed like everything was okay but that I must have had a vasovagal syncopal episode in response to the pain in my shoulder.

The doctor looked at me. She must have picked up my personality type or seen the stress in my eyes. She told me, "You're not Superwoman. I need you to get some rest and not stress." She continued to explain that most knots people experience in their shoulder and neck areas stem from too much stress and not enough rest or relaxation.

She handed me a prescription for a muscle relaxer and told me I needed to go home and do nothing. Just rest and relax. All I could think about was the amount of work I had to do that day. I'd managed to send a brief text to my managers while I waited for the test results, so they knew something was wrong.

The doctor was also smart enough to know that it was necessary to write me a doctors' note for at least three days away from work. In the past, I had to be kicked out of the office if I felt bad. Sick days weren't an option for me. There was always way too much on my to-do list. To ask me to take three days off was torture.

After leaving the clinic, I reluctantly had my mom drive me to a pharmacy, then back home. For the next three days, I lay on a twin mattress on the floor of my living room so that I could relax but still hang out with Alice and Tony.

I was forced to take a pause.

I had no idea that my stress and constant "go, go, go" attitude could reach a point that would cause me physical pain.

The American Psychological Associations' online article, "Stress Effects on the Body," states that "Chronic stress causes the muscles in the body to be in a more or less constant state of guardedness. When muscles are taut and tense for long periods of time, this may trigger other reactions of the body and even promote stress-related disorders."

After my trip to the emergency clinic, I was reminded of a previous conversation with a friend. She had told me, "You can try to act like everything's fine. You can try to be Superwoman and fake it till you make it. But, at some point, it will catch up to you." At the time, I thought I had it all figured out and would be able to handle my stress and survive off six hours or less of sleep a night.

The problem was that thought process was complete crap. I had to learn how to rest and not just by getting enough sleep. I had to learn not to be superwoman. I had to learn not to carry the full weight and responsibilities of my career, motherhood, and family on my shoulders. I had my wake-up call. My body was telling me, enough is enough, and it was time I listened.

I didn't learn my lesson right away. Since that episode, I've had four other times when I've experienced stress-induced knots in my upper back from constant worrying and putting too much on my plate. Fortunately, as soon as I feel it coming on now, I realize that I need to prescribe myself rest.

The Benefits of Rest

Anytime that the world seems to be overwhelming or when things are becoming too much to bear, my first step is always to get some rest. I can accomplish this by taking a nap or spending some time relaxing in a comfy chair or on the couch. My spiritual journey has taught me that sleep and rest equal a better mood and increased ability to handle the stress of life. I've increased my minimum to seven hours of sleep a night (normally getting a full eight), and I regularly take at least one long nap on the weekend.

Fortunately, that's been easier to achieve these last eighteen months with COVID-19 and working from home, and our camper. Going camping almost every other weekend gives me the necessary prescription of rest, nature, and family that I now know are imperative in my life. I hope to never have another vasovagal episode again. One of those lessons was enough. I also hope to never get another stress-related knot in my back or neck.

It still fascinates me that stress and lack of rest have as much power as they do on the body, despite what we try to control in our minds. To prevent that harm, we must prioritize getting a full night's sleep. We also need to take the time to rest. How many hours of sleep are you getting? Do you allow yourself to take a nap when needed?

Rest shouldn't be just for vacation or something to do when we retire. Rest needs to be a part of everyone's happiness recipe. The path to mental stability relies on it.

CHAPTER 8

THE RELEASE

———

"Peace is accepting today, releasing yesterday
and giving up the need to control tomorrow."

—LORI DESCHENE

I had gone through the years of turbulence being misdiagnosed time and time again. I was told by one doctor that I was
depressed and given antidepressants just to turn around and
be told by another that I needed anti-anxiety medication. At
one point, I was taken off all medications to only be treated
with hypnotherapy.

I was on a rollercoaster that seemed to have no end. Then
came Dr. Hauser. She is the only person outside of my inner
circle that I trust wholeheartedly with my life. It is a trust that
has been built through my trials, struggles, and successes
over the last 20 years.

Within a matter of minutes during my first session with
Dr. Hauser, I had a name for what was causing my chaos,

and by the end of that session, I also had a plan to get better. Without her help, guidance, and wisdom, I would have struggled much more than I have. I can honestly say that I don't think I would have made it out of the darkness.

Psychiatry

During the darkest point of my life, Dr. Hauser gave me a choice. I could either accept that I needed to be hospitalized and agree to receive shock therapy treatments or go back to the medication that had worked in the past, Lamictal. I had resented having to take that medication because it made me extremely sleepy. The medication also made me feel like I was walking around in a haze, almost zombie-like.

It was my choice, and she believed in me when I didn't believe in myself. She told me I was strong enough to pull myself from this darkness with the help of that medication. I didn't *need* to be hospitalized.

I listened to her and chose to go back on Lamictal. Looking back, it was one of the best decisions I've ever made.

One of her brilliant pieces of advice came when I told her about my struggles during a manic phase. I felt no need to take my medication. I told her, "It's all in my head. I feel so much better. It must have been just a phase." She then gave me the "aha" moment upon which I still reflect.

Dr. Hauser said, "If I told you, you had a heart condition, and medication was the only way to fix it so that you would live, would you take your heart medication?"

"Of course," I responded.

"Okay. What if you needed something for your liver or kidneys? Would you take that?"

"Of course."

"So why is taking medication for your brain not okay? It's just like any other organ in your body."

Bingo!

That realization was profound to me. We infrequently think of our brain as an organ, but it is. It just so happens to be one of the most important organs in our entire body. So, of course, it's understandable that at times, it may malfunction, and medication is needed to fix it in those moments.

In the article, "The Roots of Mental Illness," Thomas R. Insel, MD, former director of the National Institute of Mental Health, states, "mental illnesses are no different from heart disease, diabetes or any other chronic illness. All chronic diseases have behavioral components as well as biological components. The only difference here is that the organ of interest is the brain instead of the heart or pancreas. But the same basic principles apply."

This understanding of the brain needs to be the norm in order for the stigma surrounding mental illness to end. Then, those who struggle with mental illness will view their disease just as someone with a heart condition does.

When I had my six-month checkup call with Dr. Hauser in April of 2021, it should have lasted the usual fifteen minutes, but it ended up being almost forty-five.

I let it all out.

I was struggling at work and fighting to keep it together, personally. I felt for the first time in years that I needed to get back on medication and recognized that my recent life changes had triggered a depressive state.

She responded, "Yes, this is all situational. But the problem is, you're lacking self-confidence, and you're allowing yourself to continue to be taken advantage of at work. You have a decision to make. You can, one, stay and be miserable, or two, you can leave, move to Colorado and find another job. Option number three, you can set boundaries with your boss or, four, talk to the CEO of the company and get his take and guidance on things."

She advised option three would be extremely difficult, since I don't like confrontation and it would require me to be in a constant state of discomfort. Three out of the four options she gave me were acceptable solutions; one was not. "Doing nothing" was off the table. Something *had* to be done.

She had me schedule an appointment in a month so that I could give her a follow-up of what I had decided and the actions I had taken.

It was exactly what I needed at that moment, even though it was not what I wanted. Calling out my bluff drove me into immediate action. In the following four weeks, I took action on all three of her four acceptable options.

First, I had to decide whether to move to Colorado or stay in Texas in the home we were going to purchase from my parents. I called my realtor and had him come walk the property to get his opinion. We discussed a major remodel versus a freshening up. We also discussed just moving to Colorado and walk away from the deal my parents had offered us. Ultimately, I devised a plan to stay the course to buy the Dripping Springs house from my parents so that we could remodel it, sell it, and move to Colorado in the future with a more comprehensive safety net of finances.

I also had an honest conversation with my manager and let her know how upset I had been for the last year, especially the last few months. I felt incessantly micromanaged and that nothing we did as a team was ever enough. I also called the CEO so that I could have a chat with him the next week.

The only thing I didn't do was let it all remain the same.

The stress from being unhappy with my career affected my personal life, marriage, and parenting. That all stopped upon that video conference call with Dr. Hauser. I was no longer going to sit still and lose what was left of my self-confidence. A new fire had been started inside of me, and just coping was no longer an option.

Coaching

As an introvert and an empath, I always have a lot of anxiety going into group settings or new situations. So, after checking in and getting my name tag and course documents for the first module of coach-training certification, I bee-lined it to the drink station to make myself some tea.

While waiting for it to brew, I stood in that corner, hugging the table, taking it all in. Before learning that I was an empath, I had no idea why I always felt the need to stand in the corner and take in a room. I had always thought it was my social anxiety disorder.

Lauren walked up and introduced herself. She asked if I was from Austin and what I did for work. Talking with her instantly helped calm my nerves. At least then, I knew one person in the room.

Most people have a misunderstanding of what life coaching is truly about. It's having someone hold space for you so that you can grow and build the future you desire. Your coach is an engaged listener who allows you to work through your struggles, your problems, or desires and guides you towards what you want in your life.

A professionally trained life coach will never tell you what to do. They are there to challenge your beliefs when they impede your progress and champion you on your way to greatness. Your coach will be the greatest listener you will ever have, in tune not only with the words that you say but also with your tone and expressions. A coach is able to identify when your heart and your mind are in unison or in conflict.

The universe must have been in play because I found out a few weeks after meeting Lauren at training, she would be my coach for our first round of peer coaching. Now, over two years later, she still coaches me every other week. Having her as my coach has helped me realize many important lessons that have become my survival guide and techniques for thriving.

1. There is power in spending time alone. It's not selfish; it's a necessity.
2. I need rest.
3. Focus on my successes. Take credit for how far I've come.
4. Have a daily practice of gratitude.
5. Allow myself grace.
6. Freedom is my spirit animal.
7. Make time for my John Muir moments.
8. Let life flow.
9. When options present themselves, evaluate based on Kate's Measuring Stick.
10. Take action for the possibilities, not out of fear.

Without my coach, I would not have grown as much spiritually as I have over the last two years. She has guided me through practices that have helped me understand the "why" behind my goals so that I can take actions that align with that feeling—being aligned with my "why" leads to more positive and frequent actions towards my goals.

In coach certification training at iPEC, we learned there are two types of energy, catabolic and anabolic. Catabolic energy is draining and destructive; anabolic energy is constructive and healing. Both energies serve us in life. However, we can only be a better version of ourselves when we have more anabolic than catabolic energy. Having Lauren as my coach kept me at consistently higher levels of anabolic energy, allowing me to see obstacles as lessons and looking for the opportunity to grow.

When I forget these things, Lauren's right there to bring them back to my awareness. In the last few months, when I struggled with work and felt overwhelmed, she was there for my sessions to be my release. She listened so that I could process my feelings out loud. I could then redirect my focus on actions I could take to improve my situation, producing a more anabolic work environment going forward.

Finding Your Release

I now see Dr. Hauser only two or three times a year, usually for twenty minutes. These sessions are to make sure that I'm still feeling in control, managing my mood without medication, and getting the proper amounts of exercise, nutrition, and sleep that I need.

Dr. Hauser introduced me to meditation and mindfulness. She gave me those tools to use when the anxiety causes my thoughts to spiral or when I start to feel not worthy. She almost always has one of her dogs in the office during appointments.

As silly as it sounds, I look forward to visiting her and petting the dogs! She is very good at bringing awareness to my situations, thoughts, and emotions that aren't my truth. She expresses pride in me and makes sure I reflect on how far I've come. She challenges me to keep surviving and keep thriving. She has been my champion and a partner on my journey. I would not be where I am without her help and guidance over the years.

At one point, she told me that she was thinking about moving to a different city. Luckily for me, it was only going to be a little further of a drive. But I told her, "I don't care where you go. I'll come to see you for appointments no matter what." That includes flying in from Colorado if I have to one day.

Finding and having a doctor who truly partners with you in your mental health journey is extremely powerful. The key to having this level of support is being completely open and honest with your doctor. Don't be afraid to tell her exactly how you feel or what thoughts you have been having. You have to be able to release them. Your sessions must be a place of zero judgment where trust has been fully established.

When it comes to medications for bipolar disorder, there's one that works best for each patient. There's also a doctor who works best as well. Don't be afraid to keep seeking a doctor until you find the one that supports you, as Dr. Hauser supports me. Your doctor must be a partner in order to find stability with your mental illness.

Coaching is also a powerful tool to help you in your mental health journey. I believe it is very beneficial to have a certified coach in one's life. A coach can help you stay accountable to take action and find a way forward. A coach is a person who can help you to raise your energy levels so that you can be in the best mental state for progress.

This is why I knew I felt compelled to become a life coach. I wanted to be able to help others achieve the life of their dreams, regardless of a diagnosis. Every person should strive to be in a state of growth. That is the key to thriving with your mental illness.

CHAPTER 9

FOOTPRINTS ON MY HEART

———

"It came to me that every time I lose a dog they take a piece of my heart with them, and every new dog who comes into my live gives me a piece of their heart. If I live long enough, all the components of my heart will be dog, and I will become as generous and loving as they are."

—ANONYMOUS

When I was in my teens, my cat Fuzzy always knew when I was upset. She was a long-haired, dilute Tortie with an old soul. It didn't matter where I was in the house; she knew when I was crying or sad and would come to rub herself on my face and lie with me. It would give me a brief moment of joy and provide me with some relief I desperately needed.

The companionship that pets give us is truly unique. It's a best friend-level relationship without any judgment. Animals are full of pure love and have brought light into my life when I have found myself surrounded by darkness.

Growing up, I somehow convinced my parents to keep every stray cat that ever wandered up to our home. Most of them were pregnant or in desperate need of a vet. I would lure them in with a bowl of cat food and pick a descriptive name. There was Snapper, Tangerine, Salt & Pepper, Smokey, Dark Sun, Ripley, Alexander, and Rascal. At one point, we had thirteen cats and three dogs. I loved them all, but there have been a special few in my life who brought me the most comfort during my times of sorrow.

For my seventh birthday, I was given Blackberry, a chow chow-Labrador mix puppy rescued from the pound. She was the only black puppy in a litter of yellow and without the signature black chow tongue. She had the demeanor of a lab with a curled chow tail and had a sweet and calm disposition. She was an expert at sneaking food off the kitchen counter and daintily carrying it back to my room to devour. Her greatest find was a Mississippi Mud cake that no one noticed was missing until it was time to bring it out and sing happy birthday to my dad. The only evidence left was the glass pan licked clean lying under my bed. I guess she was immune to chocolate poisoning.

Pet rescuing has continued into my adult life. My husband Tony and I have had seven animals—four dogs and three cats. Sugar was our first pet together. She was a blue nose pit bull puppy we got together after barely dating for eight weeks. Smokey, a stray silver tabby at the vet, quickly followed. Then there was Sophie, a brown tabby kitten, rescued from a box on the side of the road—my twenty-first birthday present from Tony.

Our fourth animal together was Spanky, a pit bull puppy runt who grew into a seventy-pound love bug. He was a Momma's boy, my shadow, and a once-in-a-lifetime dog. Whenever I looked at him, I could see and feel his unconditional love. I only got to spend eleven years with him. He passed away in August of 2019 from a brain tumor.

We had always wanted to add a small dog to our pack, but the six-pound Chihuahua, Luna, was never the dog I had envisioned. A friend had brought her from Mexico for someone else, but that person had decided not to keep her. I never thought I would ever own a Chihuahua, but she had none of the typical Chihuahua behavior. She just thought she was another pit bull. Sadly, she passed away from bladder cancer in February 2021. She was only six.

One Sunday afternoon, leaving Petco, Tony was approached by an older woman in the parking lot holding a ten-day-old black and white kitten she had found in her yard. He was underweight, his eyes were crusted closed, and his legs were covered in ant bites.

Tony offered to take him since I had bottle-fed kittens before. I could take him to Century Animal Hospital the next morning, where I was still doing the bookkeeping before heading to work. The kitten could be nursed back to health and adopted. Sonny never left our family. Tony was convinced we needed to keep him since he would "complete our family: three dogs, three cats, three boys, and three girls." I guess my love for animals had rubbed off on him.

The Demise

Two weeks before Christmas 2020, I was feeling the joy that comes with the holiday season. I look forward to the last three months of every year. There's so much celebrating and family time that I can't help but feel good. I had just wrapped up my morning work conference calls when Sugar, now fourteen years old, stood up from her bed. I suddenly heard heavy panting behind me. As I spun my chair around, her back legs collapsed, splaying horizontally beneath her. Her upper body fell just as I caught her head on its way to the concrete floor.

I watched as her eyes glazed over, and she seemed to slip away. I called for Tony. He was still in our bedroom, half asleep.

He called back, not hearing exactly what I had said. Again, I calmly asked for him to come to my office and to make sure our daughter stayed behind. Confused, but hearing the tone of my voice, he came running. I sat there, on the cold, hard floor, cradling Sugar's head in my hands as she started drooling, then defecating on herself. My stomach knotted, overcome with the thought, *this is the end.*

* * *

Two years prior, I was home with our daughter, as my husband had just left to go fish the San Marcos River. Sugar had just stood up from her bed, taken a step forward, and her legs immediately splayed out beneath her.

Sugar was unconscious, her gums pale, cold, and white. She was barely breathing. Overcome with panic, I grabbed my phone, wondering how I was going to get her to the car. I needed to race to the nearest vet emergency room, but I had a young child in tow. My husband answered my call almost immediately and said he could be home in less than ten minutes.

I sat there helpless, holding Sugar in my lap on our kitchen floor. She quit breathing for what seemed like minutes, then suddenly, I noticed her chest rise slightly. Putting my hand in front of her muzzle, I felt the hot, moist air. Lifting her lip, the pale white now seemed to have a slight shade of pink.

A glimmer of hope warmed me.

The front door burst open, and within minutes, we were in the car, racing down the highway to the emergency room. It was not until after significant testing that she was diagnosed with an anaphylactic shock episode and would make a full recovery.

* * *

A little over a year after that, she also suffered what I originally thought was a stroke. She suddenly lost her ability to stand, unable to hold her own weight. Her eyes twitched left to right. It ended up being Old Dog Vestibular Disease—a condition thought to be caused by an allergy or inner ear issue. The doctor told us it causes temporary loss of motion and balance, but most dogs can make a significant recovery. Over the next month, roughly 90 percent of her abilities returned on their own.

* * *

After everything she had overcome in the last two years, here we were again.

Tony stood at the office doorway with confusion on his face. I told him to come over to hold her head and comfort her. I needed to run to the kitchen to grab paper towels and a spray bottle to clean the feces from her rear. I did not want her dying in those conditions.

Running back to the office, I was surprised to see Sugar standing, being helped back to her bed by Tony. She had suddenly popped back to life. Tony looked up at me, and we locked eyes—as if to ask *what had just happened?*

This episode, however, felt different from the two prior health scares. I feared finality.

I called the vet to see if I could bring her in for an exam. Fortunately, he could work Sugar in between appointments in the next half-hour.

While I grabbed my purse, Tony grabbed a blanket and wrapped her up, then carried her to the car. He put her in my lap, and I rushed to the vet. I held her in my arms as we waited in an exam room for the doctor. After several minutes, the vet came in to perform an exam. In the process, Sugar exhibited phantom symptoms of what the vet could only deduce was an earlier seizure.

I was faced with a tough decision; *do I play the waiting game?*

It was Friday, and the vet would be closed over the weekend, meaning a possible middle-of-the-night trip to the emergency vet. My other option: make the decision to let her go, there and then. Tony had gone to work after dropping our daughter off with family for the day. I knew he had a full day of appointments, but I could not make this decision by myself. Sugar had always been a daddy's girl.

The vet then suggested, "Why don't y'all just take the day to be with her and come back around closing?"

I hesitantly texted Tony. He would be in the middle of his first appointment that morning. I let him know that I felt it was time to let her go, and that we should take this opportunity to spend the day with her and return for her euthanasia that evening.

He agreed.

Sugar and I left the vet and drove to the barbershop to help Tony move his day's appointments. He finished with his second client, and we headed home. Sugar appeared exhausted and slept for the first hour and a half on her bed in my office.

I spent a few minutes getting everything squared away at work, then pulled a twin mattress next to Sugar's bed. I caught my mind retreating into numbness, trying to dissociate from the reality of the situation and not feel the emotional pain. However, I did not want our last moments to be her comforting me. It was my turn to give that comfort back to her. I wanted to stay strong in that moment for her.

I laid there for over an hour, watching Sugar sleep before she eventually woke up. She saw me lying on the mattress next to her and got up to stumble over so that she could bury herself under the blanket. We cuddled there together with Luna. Luna had been diagnosed with bladder cancer the month before and had only been given a couple of months to live herself.

I wanted to stay present, knowing that this was the last few hours I would ever have with Sugar. It took every ounce of energy I had left to fight back my overwhelming emotions.

We had not given her human food in over ten years. She had once battled pancreatitis after being fed some BBQ rib meat. But it was our custom for our pets to get a special treat before they departed, so Tony left to get her last meal.

Tony arrived back home with a cheeseburger and chili cheese hot dog and sat down next to us on the twin mattress.

We all lay there, surrounding each other for the last time. The minutes flew by, the hour before we needed to leave for our final goodbye approached.

We had bought her several toys and specialty dog treats two weeks earlier when she had received a diagnosis of soft tissue sarcoma in her right shoulder. We had watched it grow every day, causing her to limp more and more as the mass protruded off her shoulder.

There were two things Sugar loved to do most in this world. The first was going to the river to swim and fetch sticks. The second was fetching her ball. As it was a cold December day, we decided that going to the river one last time would not be in her best interest. Tony, Sugar, Luna, and I headed to the backyard for the next best thing.

Her morning seizure had left her wobblier than the last few months, but she still wanted nothing more than to play with her ball. We sat out on our back patio, rolling the ball only a few feet in front of her, allowing her one last time to do the thing she loved. She was still Sugar, not wanting to give us the ball back but then pushing it into our hands or legs, challenging us to tug of war. We could see her begin to tire, so Tony went inside to get the hamburger and hot dog. He cut both in half and walked back out with a plate of deliciousness. She inhaled it in a matter of seconds, as only dogs can do. I do not even think she tasted any of it.

It was time to leave for the vet, and I asked Tony if he was going to be there. This would be his first experience with euthanizing a pet, and I worried it would traumatize him. He lost his father when he was seven years old, and he hated going to doctors or hospitals for humans or pets.

He said he could not bring himself to come inside with me and would wait in the car. After pulling into the parking lot of the vet, he traded places with me in the back seat and spent his last few minutes alone, holding and comforting Sugar for the last time.

After saying his final goodbyes, Sugar and I made our way to the waiting room. For a few seconds, I could not hold back the tears. Thankfully, the technician called us into the exam room. I was able to regroup, and I laid down with Sugar on a comfortable blanket they had put on the floor.

This was not my first time letting one of my pets go. After growing up with many dogs and many more cats, it had become awfully familiar to me. I always felt it was best to stay with them in those final moments, to be strong for them so that they only felt my comfort and not my sorrow.

The technicians came in and prepped her catheter. She laid calmly next to me. The reality of the situation crept over me as I picked out the urn in which her ashes would be returned to us. Time seemed to temporarily freeze, and I suddenly felt as if I had become a spectator of this moment.

The vet came into the room and asked if I was ready to say goodbye. My head nodded reluctantly. I was conflicted in that moment, feeling like I was failing her since she was not actively dying. My heart, however, knew she was not going to get any better. That afternoon when she looked at me, I could tell she was tired. She had given everything she had these last few months to stay with us. Now, it was my time to do the last kind of thing any pet owner can do. Allow one's pet to pass as peacefully as possible without pain.

The vet administered her sedative, and she quickly fell asleep, snoring as she always did. The vet reached for the final injection, and I felt the urge to yell, "No. Never mind. Stop!" But my lips would not move. I was doing the right thing. Her breathing slowed, and I could feel her spirit leave her body. I told her one last time how much Daddy and I loved her, and the grief suddenly took its hold.

I could no longer hold back my sorrow. Tears poured down my face as I wiped away the snot running from my nose. I was conflicted by the happiness of imagining she would now get to see her brother, Spanky, again. I pictured him being there to greet her first, holding his rope, ready for the ultimate game of tug of war with her. I sat there with her alone for another minute, quietly and lovingly petting her head before walking away for the last time. I had tunnel vision walking back to the car.

Tony and I drove in silence to go pick up our daughter. I dreaded having to explain to a three year old why she would never see her dog again. When we got home, Tony knelt in front of her and calmly explained that Sugar had gotten sick, and she was not going to be with us anymore. She replied, "Where's Sugar going?" After trying to explain Heaven the best we could, he gave her a hug, and she seemed content with our response.

I had to explain it to her again, several times the next morning, and she asked at least once a day for the next few months where Shug Shug was.

Over the next few days, I stayed numb, only allowing myself to cry in the late evenings or early mornings when everyone else was asleep. We had a camping trip scheduled that weekend at McKinney Falls State Park, only a thirty-minute drive from our house. I do not remember much from that weekend. I just felt empty, grief-stricken, and unable to imagine what it would look like after fourteen years of having Sugar in our lives, marriage, and relationship. She was our first "child," but most importantly, she had been the glue in our family—our constant and loyal companion.

The following week, on a chilly Friday morning, I found myself on a walk in my neighborhood. The tip of my nose, almost certainly red, tingling like Rudolph. I felt the tears begin to gather in the corners of my eyes. My mind had wandered, thinking about the emptiness of not having Sugar with us that past week. In that moment, something shifted. I refused to look at her life as a loss. I needed to look at this as a fourteen-year life lesson.

Sugar had a spirit about her that very much reflected my own. She was a strong, independent dog, full of energy even until her last day. She had taught us responsibility and had been an ambassador against the stigma around Pitbull's. She loved children, other dogs, and her kitty brothers and sister. She always let children tug on her tail and ears or just lie all over her. She had a certain sass, yet sweetness, about her. She was a Daddy's girl who grew into her Momma's dog in the end.

Like us, Sugar enjoyed nature. She loved swimming at the river or just running in an open field. She was our family protector, and after Spanky's passing, she had replaced him as my shadow. I know in my heart that I will see her again and that she truly is happy right now, free from pain and running amuck with Spanky in heaven. I take comfort knowing we have gained another angel to watch over us and to hold forever in our hearts.

Our Doggy Angels

Losing our three dogs over a period of a year and a half was one of the hardest things I had to endure in my adult life to this point. There are no words for the amount of grief I have felt for them. The worst part has been watching Alice, still crying over the passing of Luna, now eight months later. It's hard for a four-year-old to grasp the permanence of death. The only way I have been able to provide Alice comfort in her loss is by explaining that Luna, Sugar, and Spanky are always with her. They're just memorialized in her heart now. It's true what they say: the pain never goes away; you just learn to move forward and live with it.

Yes, they were animals. But, to me, they were my first children. They were a source of strength when I felt I had none left. They live in a constant state of joy. My dogs never seemed to have a bad day. In times where I haven't had the strength to take care of myself, I've always had my animals' needs to pull me into action. Their sole reliance on me for their most basic of needs has always been a motivator. I may not have had the strength to make food for myself, but I always found the energy to care for them.

A pet can be a constant companion when you find yourself all alone. You can tell a pet your joys, troubles, and deepest darkest secrets without ever feeling judged. They love you regardless.

Our pets teach us many things, but mostly they teach us how to love unconditionally and how to never let a bad moment ruin our day. They are perfect examples of how to live without judgment and always be in the moment. It doesn't matter who you are, what disease you may have, or where you are from. You are their everything.

It's true what they say. We don't deserve the unwavering love our pets provide, but I am so thankful they so freely give it. Our pets are our opportunity to learn to live life wholeheartedly. If only we all lived life as they do. How different would our world be?

There are so many animals that need a loving home. Consider rescuing a pet if you don't have one in your life. Owning a pet is a big responsibility, but in return, you get a loving friend who is always there when you need them. Pets are a support system on standby at home every day.

We love you, Sugar Bear, Spanky Doodle, and Luna Lu. We will see you again.

CHAPTER 10

A CHANGE OF PACE

"When you arise in the morning, think of what a precious privilege it is to be alive, to breathe, to think, to enjoy, to love."

—MARCUS AURELIUS

By May 2020, my family had been at home for two months and counting due to statewide quarantine. Like many others, my everyday shifted from a long commute and spending structured days at work in an office, to rolling out of bed to work ten-to-twelve-hour days virtually from home. The norm of spending the majority of time away at work and only having a couple of hours to see my daughter each day was replaced with my daughter coming in and out of my make-shift home office all day long.

Before the quarantine started, I had been asked to oversee an additional larger team after their manager was let go.

I was on a path towards exhaustion, fueled only by the appreciation of having a job after seeing several coworkers were furloughed. We were all, collectively, just trying to keep the company in business.

I only left the house to pick up our scheduled curbside grocery order that had to be placed two weeks prior and to take evening walks with my daughter to look for painted rocks around our neighborhood. I was caught in a whirlwind of joy, getting to spend so much time at home, and burnout from being "plugged in" to work for all hours of the day. After we realized that this was not going to be the "couple weeks" at home everyone initially expected, Tony and I agreed that we were probably looking at this lifestyle for the foreseeable future.

Taking a Risk & Fulfilling a Vision

A few weeks later, on our way to pick up our weekly grocery order, we passed a local RV dealership. Tony casually mentioned maybe now would be a good time to buy that RV we had wanted. I had been looking wistfully at the RV dealer at that moment. We had dreamed about getting a travel trailer for years, especially when we had been on vacations in Colorado and Yellowstone, our most memorable vacation of all.

Now seemed like a perfect opportunity for a lifestyle change. As long as I had internet, I could work from anywhere. A change of scenery could also help me wind down from the demands of working frantically from home all day.

Over the next few weeks, the topic kept coming up in conversation. It seemed the universe was in favor of our idea as well, seeing as every time I turned on the TV to watch my usual travel channel, a new RV series was on. One Sunday morning, we decided on a whim that we would go look at a dealership in the area.

That day, a nice, upbeat salesman greeted us and asked us about features we were looking for and if we were open to looking at used travel trailers. There was one left on the lot that was less than a year old and in our exact price range.

I suddenly felt butterflies of excitement as I realized its paint job perfectly complimented our truck that we would use to tow it. It was primarily grey with accent colors of black and the same shade of navy blue. I opened the door to find the exact floor plan that I considered the best match for our family. The interior color scheme was also the same as my online favorites, and after looking it over inside and out, it seemed as if we were looking at a brand-new unit.

Reluctant to think we had found "the one" on our first try, we asked to look at a new model. It didn't feel the same. I asked Tony if we were ready to start this new journey. He replied, "I think we are finally ready."

"Okay, let's do this!" I said enthusiastically.

We headed back into the sales office. After filling out the initial paperwork, we were scheduled for the final purchase and walk-through that Friday, coincidently the day before our ninth wedding anniversary.

The next week, our entire evenings were spent watching online RV beginner videos and making our list of must-have supplies. We did not, however, think to book a reservation for our first camping trip coming that weekend.

Friday finally arrived, and I had my bi-weekly call with my coach, Lauren, from the dealership parking lot before our appointment. I realized during the session that part of the five-year vision I had written the year before in an exercise for coach training was coming to fruition. I had envisioned we would have a travel trailer that would allow us to take weekend trips around Texas in order to spend as much time as possible in nature.

The sudden work-style change brought on by COVID-19 was making it possible.

As we concluded the coaching session, I set the intention to take full advantage of this newfound opportunity to travel and be in nature.

We spent over three hours with a specialist who walked through each and every switch, appliance, and feature the travel trailer had. We purchased the necessary supplies from our list at their onsite shop, and the final test was to safely hook the RV to our truck. We were ready to start our new journey that anniversary weekend.

The only question was, where? I searched online for campsites for hours that evening with no luck. I was able to book a lakeside site for the following weekend, at Inks Lake State Park. Coincidentally, as a child, Tony had spent many summers camping at Inks Lake with his uncle and family in their travel trailer. It seemed like the perfect place for our maiden voyage and was only an hour and a half drive from our house.

Not deterred, we decided that although we were not going to be able to take the RV out that weekend, we would still celebrate by having our anniversary dinner curbside, in front of our home. Our usual anniversary meal of Salt Lick BBQ would not be possible since the restaurant was temporarily closed due to COVID-19, so we settled on takeout from a local Chinese restaurant and celebrated with a bottle of champagne after our daughter went to bed.

We spent the whole meal discussing our disbelief that we had finally pulled the trigger and made the purchase during a global pandemic. Tony was not even working since bar-bershops were closed statewide. We had taken a huge finan-cial risk by putting a large amount of money down for the down payment, while our monthly income was down over fifty percent.

The only thing that mattered to us was the time we were going to spend together as a family in that travel trailer and the memories that we were going to create with our daughter.

A Change of Pace

Now, over eighteen months from the start of our RV journey, we have gone to eighteen different state parks on twenty-six weekend-long trips. We've taken two separate week-long trips up to Colorado and down to Big Bend. For us, buying this travel trailer has really been the best thing to come out of the COVID-19 pandemic.

We can get out and be in nature and explore what is all around us. We have a new appreciation for the state parks of Texas, previously unexplored.

When we are camping, time slows down. I am able to stay fully present and "in the moment" on our trips. The stress and worries of the previous week disappear. I make a point to book a spot that is near trees so that I can lay for periods of time in my hammock, reading or resting. My hammock is my happy place.

We have been able to retreat from this pandemic and spend much of our time amidst the chaos and uncertainty around us, grounded and content. It is our little personal getaway that warms my soul every time I see the camper parked in front of our home, ready to head out on another adventure. Every time I open the door and walk inside, I feel the same excitement I felt that first day on the RV lot, and I fall in love with the camper over and over again.

We dream of one day being able to leave for months at a time to explore the nature around our country. For now, we will be "weekend warriors." Or, should I say, "weekend wanderers?"

Changing pace doesn't have to be drastic or constant. One can start with just a day a month and gradually work towards more. The important thing is to escape the rat race and the constant need to be on the go. Make sure you change the normal rhythm of your life. That's where the calm is, and the adventure begins.

Despite the financial challenges we were experiencing, and the complete unknown of what COVID-19 was going to bring, I am incredibly grateful that we took the chance. We chose to do something extraordinary for our family. The trips have given us memories to last a lifetime, helped us capture thousands of invaluable snapshots, and honored my values of family and nature.

CHAPTER 11

MOTHER NATURE

"In every walk in nature, one receives
far more than he seeks."

—JOHN MUIR

John Muir is my spiritual guide. I strive to have the depth of connection with nature and the mountains that he did. Often called the father of national parks, he advocated for preserving the wilderness that we now get to experience in our state and national parks.

The idea of walking out into nature and seeing where your footsteps take you, for however long, appeals to me. Everyone can find this meditative space in one form or another. There is so much to learn about oneself from nature.

Lake of Many Rocks

It was a cold September morning at Rocky Mountain National Park in Colorado. I made sure to wear multiple layers, and I brought all my camera gear in the new belt I bought for our first out-of-state RV trip. It allowed me to have all my camera lenses easily accessible. I had my backpack loaded with water, snacks, and essential items for a hike in the wilderness. I started on the hike, excited there were not too many people out yet. Since the trail is so popular, I left early in an effort to get some of it to myself.

This particular hike meanders up in elevation as you pass four different alpine lakes. Shortly before the third lake, there is a split in the trail to Lake Haiyaha.

As I arrived at Nymph Lake, the second lake on the trail, I pulled out my camera to take my first pictures of the morning. My camera screen would not turn on. I realized, despite all my preparation that morning, I had left the camera battery charging in the truck.

I stood there, disappointment quickly turning to frustration. I had to decide if it was worth it to go back to the truck. It would mean a loss of forty-five minutes or more, and I had a deadline. Once I got back from my trek, we would have to get the trailer ready and make our way back to Amarillo, a nine-hour drive pulling the RV.

In that moment of frustration, I made a choice.

I chose to let it go. I realized that the purpose of that hike for me was to be in the moment with Mother Nature and recharge. By not having my camera, I would reclaim the pure experience of my journey, rather than worrying about getting the perfect shot or looking at things from a photographer's perspective. I left behind the frustration and disappointment; instead, I chose to hike forward.

I made my way up to the split in the trail. The path on the right would take me to Dream and Emerald Lakes; the one on the left led to Lake Haiyaha. I decided to make a quick stop at Dream Lake for a chance to take in the view before the typical crowd of people arrived. After a few minutes of hiking, I reached the edge of the lake, took out my phone, snapped a quick photo, and then paused to take in the beauty. I turned and headed back to the split for Lake Haiyaha.

At the time, I did not know the extent of the elevation gain for the coming stretch of my journey. After passing the split, the trail almost immediately started an upward incline to a long switchback. There were several areas where the snow had turned to patches of ice, and I was thankful to have my trekking poles.

After the switchback, I was rewarded with a breathtaking panoramic view from the side of the mountain. There was a slight haze in the air from a wildfire currently burning on the other side—just outside of the park. Fortunately, there had been a snowstorm the day before our arrival, which drastically reduced the smoke in the air until that morning.

In the distance, I could see our campground next to Sprauge Lake, the road I had driven that morning, the meadows below, and Nymph Lake. The trail's edge dropped off down the mountainside, filling me, for a moment, with my fear for heights. After taking in the magnificent vista and catching my breath, I continued my journey, passing the first group of people I had seen since the split.

I was nearing the end of the trail when it turned into a field of rocks and boulders. The lake had been formed by a glacier. Now, just a small patch of ice remained at the very top of the mountain ridge that surrounded the lake. The glacial movement had left behind huge boulders and rocks that hikers could spend hours exploring around the lake. The rocks give the trail its Native American name: "Haiyaha."

After a brief period of bouldering, I came to a beautiful tree. There are a few trees around the lake that are hundreds of years old, with trunks twisted over time from the harsh winds sweeping down the mountain. The setting appeared ancient—as if frozen in time.

From there, I carefully made my way down the boulders to the lake's edge. There was a large boulder sticking out of the water. I looked down around its edge, and I could see straight down, rock after rock below me, the water clear as glass.

I sat down, the only person at the lake, surrounded by pure, raw, beautiful nature. It was my little slice of heaven. I kept looking all around me, left to right, over and over, just taking in the towering mountains, splashed with snow, almost completely surrounding the lake. I could see what was left of the glacier directly in front of me. A slight cold wind blew across the lake. The sky, a light blue, was absent of clouds, and the morning sun was shining. *Perfection.*

In that moment, I felt whole, connected to something greater. I had tapped into the source, overwhelmed by the genuine appreciation of the journey I have been on to reach the point I am now. That is what I seek the most, the oneness, the wholeness, the interconnectedness, not just between me and others, but between me and nature. That connection with Mother Nature, the Universe, God, whatever you call it, is for me what life is truly about and leaves me feeling worthy, absent from any judgment.

Even though I am not able to sit on top of that boulder every day, I do have the power at any moment to bring myself back to that experience in my mind. I can close my eyes and visualize, wherever I am, that feeling of connectedness and peace. It allows me to come back from what I am dwelling on or when I feel like I may not be on the "right" path. To move me again out of my mind and into my heart. It reminds me that sometimes things don't go as planned, but that it doesn't have to ruin the moment.

Connecting with Nature in the Every Day

Living in Central Texas means I'm far from the mountains. On those days when I am yearning for a hike in my beloved Rockies, I turn to one of my favorite documentaries, *Mile, Mile and a Half*. It documents a group of friends' journey on the John Muir Trail, a 210-mile hike through the Sierra Mountain range.

Fortunately for me, the hikers in the documentary are talented artists who capture the landscape beautifully with their photography and videography. Their personalities are fun, grounded, and full of connection. No matter how many times I've watched it, it still inspires me and allows me to appreciate nature's beauty, even when I'm doing daily chores.

On most days, for me, being in nature means watching the birds from my desk flitter around my backyard or the clouds move and change from my hammock. It's when I'm on a walk around my neighborhood that I stop and admire a flower or watch the deer graze. On great days, it means taking a hike in a state park on our RV adventures.

Nature teaches us about the importance of connection, purpose, respect, balance, perseverance, beauty, and change. Nature is full of ebbs and flows. Each season has a purpose and balances the whole. Much like our lives, there will be good times and bad; if you're able to recognize the importance of both, their power over you vanishes. Low points in our lives give way for growth and transformation.

My goal is to, one day, be able to walk out my front door and venture into nature for as long as I please like John Muir so often did. For now, I stay mindful in the moments that I do have and make sure I always have a plan for returning to the mountains.

"The mountains are calling, and I must go."

—JOHN MUIR

CHAPTER 12

THAT LITTLE VOICE INSIDE

———

> "Follow your heart and intuition. They somehow already know what you truly want to become. Everything else is secondary."
>
> —STEVE JOBS

In June 2019, I had received a big promotion that came with all the salary and benefits I would ever need to support my family. The thought of walking away from it was terrifying. I'd spent the last twelve years building what I thought was my lifelong career but became shackled to the golden handcuffs of my job. I had climbed up the corporate ladder, but it had left me feeling empty inside.

In the two years after my promotion, I had found myself called regularly by my intuition. That little voice deep inside pushed me to feel I was meant for more. It kept reminding me that I had a purpose, and I needed to go for it. The voice inside got louder and louder the more I'd grown spiritually and learned to listen through meditation and coach training. I wanted to help others through coaching, but that felt like I would be starting over in my professional career.

Each one of us has a purpose, and our intuition tries to guide us down that path. Unfortunately, we've grown as a society to learn to suppress it and keep it quiet.

Why?

Because the message that little voice tells us usually scares the bejesus out of us—because it involves *change*.

A Change in the Tide

In March 2020, I took the day off for my daughter's birthday and was spending it at a local park with her and my husband. It was going to be a day of dual celebration because I had received an email that morning that I'd passed my coaching certification final exam and was officially a certified professional coach. It was also the first day my company was working from home for the quarantine.

The problem was that tiny voice inside me kept calling for me to make a change. I had constant thoughts of Colorado and the urge to move there. Tony and I had talked about it since the day we honeymooned in Estes Park ten years before. *How could I make such drastic change when there were still so many unknowns in the world with the pandemic?*

I pushed down the little voice, and I tried my best to ignore it. That tortured me for months until we decided to set a date of May 2021 for our move to Colorado. It would be our tenth anniversary present to each other.

In September 2020, one of my colleagues and friends from coaching certification messaged me that a book program at Georgetown University had an enrollment period coming up for new authors. I took it as a sign and submitted my application to get into the program.

I took my initial book exploration call on the road during our RV trip to Colorado. It felt serendipitous. I didn't know what that *something* would be, but it gave me hope again.

There were weekly sessions for the book writing program, and I began writing stories that evolved into chapters. Our first draft manuscript deadline was March 2021. The first several months of writing came easy, and I was able to devote at least one full day each weekend to writing and editing, but as the deadline approached, I found small barriers popping up.

In November, while still feeling compelled by my intuition to move to Colorado, my parents offered an opportunity to buy their house in Dripping Springs, TX. It was in a great school district and would allow us to put in some sweat equity by buying the house and remodeling it over time.

After many conversations, Tony and I decided it would be worth putting our dream of Colorado on hold for now. I pushed down that little voice inside. I started calling banks and getting pre-approvals for mortgages and planned a date for the move to the house. Before we moved in, my parents would move to their second home on the other side of Austin, which had been on the market for two years with no offers.

My parents scheduled their move, and as the moving date grew closer, they unexpectedly received an offer on their second house and decided that they needed to stay in their home in Dripping Springs. It was devastating. Tony and I had finally felt like things were falling into place and felt good about the change we were going to make.

What do we do now? Do we go back to our original idea of finding a place to move to in Colorado?

It just didn't feel right this time. My gut wasn't telling me to move anymore. The disappointment of the deal with my parents falling through took the wind from our sails, and at the same time, things at work started taking their toll. Burnout was setting in.

It was the end of November, and my mom called while we were camping at Palmetto State Park. Their buyer had backed out at the last possible hour on the contract. She was in shock, but at the end of the conversation, she asked, "Would y'all want to go back to the original plan?"

I was caught off guard.

I replied, "I don't know what to think. It's still too raw. I would need to talk to Tony."

She responded, "Well, I haven't even told Dad the news yet. We can talk about it later."

After several long discussions over the next few weeks, Tony and I both committed to moving to Dripping Springs and, again, set a date.

Getting COVID-19

Three weeks before we were scheduled to move, in February, I woke up in the middle of the night with a sore throat and chills.

Tony had complained of not feeling well the afternoon before and felt like he had a fever. He decided to sleep in the spare bedroom in case it was a cold or something worse.

By the time I woke up the following morning, I had the worst sinus pressure I'd ever experienced. I knew immediately, the virus we had been diligently protecting ourselves from for over a year was here.

I found a COVID-19 testing center that had availability later that morning, so Tony and I got dressed, masked up, and drove to the clinic. Tony hates going to the doctor, and since I knew what to expect, having been tested before, I went in first. After a quick swab, I headed back out to the car to wait on the results, and Tony went in to get his test. He was immediately met at the door and taken aside by the technician I had just seen. My test had already come back positive.

We both had it.

Talk about the worst timing. We spent the next week stuck on the roller coaster of COVID-19, experiencing every possible symptom. The following week, we fought to regain our strength and our breath, all the while trying to pack our belongings.

What we didn't know, though, was that Texas was heading into one of the worst winter storms the state had ever experienced. We spent five days trapped inside our home during what Texans later dubbed *SnowVID*.

We hadn't been able to go to the grocery store since we had spent the last two weeks in quarantine but managed to get a small delivery at home right before the storm hit. It was Valentine's weekend, and temperatures stayed below freezing, even making it to the single digits. For three straight days, we had several inches of snowfall. The Texas power grid failed. We were fighting to keep the house at a tolerable temperature during rolling blackouts and had to boil water to drink.

To top it off, Tony had planned on a puppy for a Valentine's Day surprise, and his friend drove through the worst of the storm to drop him off. I figured if the puppy needed a home that bad that day, it was better off with us.

For some crazy reason, we thought it would still be a good idea to keep the same date for moving to the new house that following Saturday morning. It was just the first day most cars were able to get back on the roads, and our friends showed up bright and early.

In less than two hours, the vehicles were packed, and we arrived at the new house, having to scrape the snow and ice from the driveway to even get the trucks down to unload. Three hours later, we had everything inside, only putting together the beds as exhaustion set in.

Book Deadline

Before I knew it, the deadline for my manuscript was a week away, and only about 30 percent of it was complete. I was in a panic.

What was I going to do? How was I going to finish it?

I was at my wit's end and felt like my world was crumbling. *Can't I get a break?*

It didn't help that work was also a complete struggle. I was being smothered by micromanagement. My manager's apparent mistrust in how I did anything triggered anger and frustration.

Our Chihuahua, Luna, had terminal cancer, and I knew her time with us was coming to an end.

The next morning, we noticed water leaking from the closet in the garage that contained the water softener. The freeze had shattered the condensate drain line from the water heater and had been dripping down the wall ever since.

Something had to give, or I was going to break. Fortunately, my editor knew what I had just been through and told me I had the option to push back my book deadline. I could enroll in a bridger program group which would extend my publishing date by four months.

The stubbornness in me wanted to just push through and finish it. But then came more roadblocks.

The vet confirmed that our dog Luna's condition had worsened, and we needed to make the decision to let her go. The stress again crippled me with another knot in my back. I was confined to my bed, unable to move for several days.

After all that, I was still resistant to the idea of postponing my book. I felt like a failure, but after phone calls with my mom, sister, coach, and two of my friends, I let my editor and publisher know I would need to move my publishing date and extend my deadline for my first draft of the manuscript.

I spent the next couple of weeks defeated, with very little energy or emotion. With all the stress in the prior month, I had entered a depressive period and found myself unmotivated and resisting writing.

The situation at work got worse, and it felt unbearable to have to continue there. Each day, the fight with my depression got harder and harder. I struggled with putting my game face on and going through the motions of the day. I knew my time at that company was coming to an end. I could no longer ignore it or put up with that toxic environment. I knew what I was going to have to do, but my financial gremlin again tried to shackle me back to the golden handcuffs.

There was comfort and consistency there, but my intuition was telling me I needed to go. But *what would I do next?*

The subtle voice inside had been telling me for years that there was something greater for me to contribute to this world. Learning about life coaching in the podcast I had listened to almost four years before was the only time I felt like I knew what that "something" was. Starting a coaching practice would mean starting back at square one, but I'd been brave enough to enroll and finish my certification. *Why were the next steps so difficult?*

The answer: my financial gremlin.

The Solution

I wanted to be an entrepreneur so that I could help people, especially those on their own journey with finding stability in life with a mental illness. I wanted to work for myself and have my efforts directly drive success in my career, but the fear crippled me every time I stopped to visualize what that would look like.

COVID-19 didn't help matters either, as it further intensified the power of the golden handcuffs, especially after losing the portion of my salary when the pandemic started and when Tony wasn't able to work. I'd always been the breadwinner of the family, and I had no idea how I would ever be able to achieve professional fulfillment while still financially providing for my family.

The only good event in that period of time was that we were able to get our house sold without fixing it up or spending any time or energy getting it ready to go on the market. We had contacted our realtor on a Tuesday, and by Friday, it was on the market for sale. We received multiple offers and even got one that was over the listing price.

Two weeks went by, and we were a week away from closing and about to start our week-long RV trip to Big Bend. I got a call from our realtor that the buyer's financing had fallen through, and we wouldn't be closing that Friday. Again, I was devastated.

The one good thing had gone bad, but I didn't want it to ruin our trip.

Miraculously, two hours later, the realtor called back to say he had a potential buyer, and he was on his way to show them the house. He said he felt like he could get an offer for the same amount. An hour after that, he called to let me know the buyers loved it and would be putting in an offer that day.

Finally, a glimmer of hope shined through!

We closed on the house just two weeks after our original closing date, but I still had not made much progress on my book. Things at work had reached a breaking point for me.

But I finally had a solution. The real estate sellers' market boom had allowed us to walk away with a sizable amount of proceeds. It was the cushion I needed to feed my financial gremlin. I'd be able to cut the handcuffs, leave my job, and fulfill my purpose.

The problem was that when the money finally hit the bank account, fearfulness instead of freedom gripped me. The reality of it all and the risk sank in. I finally had the protective cushion of monetary support that would allow me to walk away from my job and be fine, but I was more terrified than I had ever been of leaving.

The fear was overwhelming, and it began to consume me. I found myself obsessing about it for days. However, it's funny how the universe works. I discovered that sometimes if you're not willing to do it yourself, the universe will do it for you.

I asked for a call with all three of my managers so that I could talk about my struggles and feelings with the current management style. During that call, I was honest about my experiences but felt like there was a lack of awareness and understanding from their sides as to why I felt that way. I was asked to bring it up whenever it happened again so that I could build awareness around the behavior with my managers.

I also decided to go meet that next Friday morning with the CEO, to ask his advice for how to be a better manager myself. I thought if I could communicate the status of progress and projects differently with my team and managers, the micromanaging I was experiencing would lessen, and I would feel differently about staying there. I knew my meeting with the CEO would ruffle some feathers. I never expected an email I sent later that afternoon to be the final nail in the coffin.

While I had been meeting with him, a series of emails from one of my managers to a team member had transpired that I felt blurred the levels of management. An error in an amount transmitted to a vendor had occurred, and a simple correction was needed. I felt it could have been easily communicated down to me to work with the team member to correct, instead of the fourteen back and forth emails that provided a proposed solution that wasn't consistent with how we'd corrected errors of that nature before. I saw it as the perfect opportunity to build awareness with my manager around the actions that were contributing to my frustrations.

I sat for the next half-hour, drafting an email explaining how communication and direction should have been delivered to me directly instead of through my team. I made sure to keep it as free of emotion as possible. I just wanted it to be my perception of the series of events. My manager's response back shocked me. I had set a new boundary and built awareness around why I was feeling micromanaged, but it had triggered a catabolic reaction.

My manager wanted to meet that following Monday in person to discuss the email. I did not. After back and forth texts and calls with my other managers over the weekend, I agreed. My only condition was to have my two other managers present in that meeting.

Unfortunately, the one who I needed to be there to support me the most, my direct manager, was not allowed in. The conversation was doomed from the start. It started with my printed email being placed in front of me. Then I was asked what reaction I expected when I had hit send. I was learning that there would be no change to the situation. You can share your opinions and set new boundaries with others, but they have to be willing to listen and desire to change their own behavior. It solidified the fact that I knew I could not work there any longer.

There would be no going back after the conversations that had transpired. And certainly no healing.

The Next Chapter

In the following weeks, I started seeing "angel numbers" multiple times a day. A fellow coach had told me that whenever consecutive single digits appear (e.g., 111 or 222), the universe is speaking to you, and each set of numbers represents a different message.

They appeared in street addresses while on walks or driving. I saw them when I checked my phone for the time or even in the phone numbers of telemarketers. My morning spirit card readings kept hinting at a change ahead. The change would be difficult but would connect me to my purpose.

The voice that I'd been trying to mute and keep quiet wasn't subtle anymore. It became so loud and strong that I couldn't imagine doing anything else. It was my time. I needed to take the leap, and the universe clearly had my back.

Over the next four months, I attended an eight-week-long group coaching program designed to help me launch my coaching practice. I submitted my first manuscript draft, switched my focus to building my audience, and then to revising my book after getting back my first round of edits. I picked a date to leave the corporate world and started to mentally prepare for the shift that I had coming.

I felt my energy shift from darkness into a more constant state of light. I was still scared, but it was getting easier and easier to see the opportunity ahead of me. Little by little, I trusted that voice inside more, and my fear lessened. Instead of that voice feeling like a constant nag, it began to feel like a trusted compass.

In coach training at iPEC, our trainers would remind us to trust the process. I was now trusting my process. All the events that had transpired over the last year had been preparing me for my next chapter. I had learned how to connect and listen to my inner voice, despite how much fear I felt. The more I had resisted it, the more struggle I had in my life. Once I accepted and aligned with it, the path ahead of me fell into place.

What has the little voice inside of you been nudging you to do? Have you been silencing it or learning to listen? I believe we all have a greater purpose and are made for more. We just have to learn to trust our soft voice inside. It is the guiding light to our highest potential.

CHAPTER 13

DAILY RITUALS

———

"Great things are done by a series
of small things brought together."

—VINCENT VAN GOUGH

What eight-year-old kid do you know that comes home, starts her homework, and stays at her desk until it's done?

My mother said I had the best study habits back in elementary. For the long drive home from school, my dad would stop so that I could get a whole French baguette and Dr. Pepper from Texas French Bread. Once home, I would run up the stairs to my room and sit down at my desk to start my homework without prompting.

I have been called a creature of habit a lot in my life. For years before it closed, I would eat lunch every Tuesday at Lulu B's, a local Vietnamese food trailer in Austin. My order was always tofu summer rolls and a tofu banh mi with an extra peanut sauce for dipping.

The same could be said of my morning smoothie; it is always made up of the same delicious ingredients every day. I follow the training guide for my runs exactly as structured and use the same order of card decks for my morning spirit readings. I thrive when I have dedicated time filled with things that bring me joy each day.

These rituals fell to the wayside with the freedom that comes with college and young adulthood. It was not a coincidence that this was when I was struggling the most with my mental health.

Reconnecting with Joyful Ritual

In my late twenties, I felt like I could not take time to do daily rituals that made me happy. I had to wake up, get dressed and fight traffic for an hour just to get to work and constantly jump from task to task all day. Then it was another hour of traffic home so that I could make dinner, do the dishes, and get ready to go to bed, just to do it all over again the next day. I had the same boring routine every day, centered around work.

Nine years into this grind, during a weekend training module for coaching, I was reminded of the importance of having a daily ritual. A ritual meant time in my day that focused on replenishing myself and creating joy. During the grind, I had forgotten the importance of prioritizing things that would fill my cup and protect my mental health so that I could, in turn, be there for others. Taking time for myself felt selfish, but I wondered if it was actually a vital element to mental stability.

In a coaching session during June 2020, I decided I would start practicing a morning ritual to combat the feeling I had of impending burnout. I desperately needed a plan to start my day on a positive note and protect my energy. I've always been more of a morning person. I enjoy the quiet when waking up early, before the others. There's a certain stillness and calm that's been brought from the night. My homework from that session was to figure out what things I really liked and wanted to incorporate into my morning ritual.

A daily ritual doesn't mean that you need to plan every minute of your day. You just need to have dedicated time that consists of things you love, things that bring you joy or ground you, and practices that replenish your inner self.

In the evening after my session that day, I sat down and began to list ideal practices I wanted to incorporate into my mornings.

- Meditation was something that I'd never been able to practice consistently. I only used it as needed, especially when my mind was overwhelmed by racing thoughts. I had long known the benefits and science behind its daily practice, so it immediately was my first item added to the list.
- A fellow coach had recently recommended I get an animal spirit card deck and do a reading every day. At first, I was a little apprehensive about using spirit cards. Initially, I thought they were dark or evil energy, like what I had grown up thinking about Tarot cards or fortune-telling. However, she had explained it was more about connecting with our angels or spirit guides who help us navigate our path in life. I decided to order a deck and added a card reading to the morning ritual list as well.
- I also love to have a candle burning while I work or relax. I have to admit I've always been a little bit of a pyromaniac and love to just sit and watch a flame burn. It's very soothing to me, and the pleasant smell of a candle is an

added bonus. It made sense to add this to the top of the list before I started meditation.

- I have never liked the taste of coffee but was introduced by my mother to what I like to call "fake coffee." My obsession started out with the Maxwell House version of powdered creamer, chocolate, and a dash of coffee, but after trying to limit processed ingredients, I have found my Starbucks Instant Mocha Latte packets. I had tried to deny the urge for a daily cup for years, but in considering my list, a cup made from half a packet seemed like a reasonable compromise in order to bring me joy, so on the list it went.
- Exercise was something else that I'd struggled with doing consistently, despite again knowing the benefits received from as little as half an hour per day. The problem was, I had the limiting belief that walks didn't count. *That's totally not true.* Since I hadn't been able to commit to daily running or some form of intense cardio during quarantine, I talked myself into the new belief that a daily walk would be sufficient.

By this point, I felt like I had a good list started. I decided to leave my notepad open on my desk with these five items so that every morning when I woke up and came to my desk to start working, I would be reminded to first go through my rituals.

My First Ritual Attempt

Fast forward nine months, and I was still working from home during the pandemic. I would wake up, roll out of bed, and head to my home office. The order and timeline of my list had been altered a bit, but I always started by pulling out that spirit animal card deck. I would take a deep breath, ask myself how I was feeling about the day, and begin to shuffle.

I reflected on the thoughts that had been on my mind the most in the last twenty-four hours or questions that I had unanswered. I would split the deck into three separate piles, close my eyes, take a deep breath, and then stack the piles together in random order. The top card from the pile was the one for the day.

The crazy thing is, every card I have pulled since I started these readings has been spot on for my life that day. I look at it as connecting to things greater than me that help me on my path. I'd transitioned from not being a very religious person to a very spiritual person, and my morning card reminds me of how we are all part of something greater.

After the reading, I would light my candle and make my morning cup of "fake coffee." I would sip on it during my morning check-in calls for work, and then it was time for my smoothie. *It's always great to start my day off with a heavy dose of plant-based nutrition.* I would get back to work, and after Tony and Alice left for the day, I would take a break and go for a morning walk or run. I almost always listened to a self-help audiobook during my walks. It was just another morning "pick me up" and a way to stay mindful.

The rest of my day was pretty much unscripted, except for meditation in the afternoons when I began to feel the need for a mental energy boost. Each evening at 9:30, my alarm went off to remind me to practice daily gratitude. I either thought of something that I was grateful for from my day or wrote down something I had accomplished in my journal. It was yet another way to end on a positive note, no matter how far I'd strayed or how down my emotional energy was.

My morning ritual had become more of a practice in the art of preparing for battle each day. My ritual was my way of putting on my battle armor in a feeble attempt to ward off the toxic energy of my work. It served its purpose, but once the stress of the move, the book, and my depressive period began, my ritual felt more like another item on my to-do list. The joy of it was lost, and I stopped the practice.

My New Ritual

It wasn't until I made the decision to quit the corporate world that I began to practice my daily rituals again. Without them, I was drained, and my inner cup was empty. I was preparing for the transition into my new working life as an author and coach. I wanted to make sure I entered this new period refreshed and recharged.

The weekend before my first week of corporate freedom, I knew I needed to create my ideal day for my next journey and bring back joy into my daily routine. This time, it wouldn't just be a ritual I did in the morning. I wanted to live my best day, all day, every day. My best day would be one full of purpose, where I have a balance of mind, body, and spirit throughout.

Here's my next attempt at my daily ritual.

Wake-up: 6 a.m.
Meditate: 6:10–6:30 a.m.
Get Alice Ready for School/Drop Off: 6:30–7:15 a.m.
Exercise: 7:15–8 a.m.
Breakfast 8–8:30 a.m.
Spiritual Time: 8:30–9 a.m.

Shower/Dress: 9–9:30 a.m.

Writing: 9:30–11 a.m.

Lunch: 11:00–11:30 a.m.

Coaching: 11:30 a.m.–2 p.m.

Pick up Alice/Business Admin: 2–3 p.m.

Dedicated 1 on 1 Time with Alice: 3–4 p.m.

Chores/Social Media: 4–5 p.m.

Family Time—Dinner/Alice's Bath/Reading: 5–10 p.m.

Bedtime: 10 p.m.

I didn't have one day in my first week of corporate freedom that followed this routine. Monday was spent wrapping up items for work and attending a going-away lunch. Tuesday, I helped my dad deliver the last of my parents' things to Goodwill from their most recent move and had lunch with him. Wednesday, Tony and I went to Pedernales State Park and hiked until it was time to pick up Alice.

I had four meetings on Thursday for the book and coaching and then booked an impromptu trip to Colorado for my birthday. I did a long run for my first week of marathon training on Friday morning and then went to a celebratory lunch with my coach.

I found myself grumpy and resentful in the evenings, and I was full of anxiety and fear. All these things should have brought me joy—but they didn't. This was not what I had planned in my new routine.

Friday evening, while lying in bed reflecting on what had gone wrong that week, I realized I was "upper limiting" myself. I chuckled because I had just read about "upper limiting" in Gay Hendricks book, *The Big Leap*, which I had received as a gift from my group coaching program.

According to Hendricks' book, upper limiting is when our "inner thermostat setting, that determines how much love, success, and creativity that's rightfully ours, prevents us from living in the ultimate destination, the Zone of Genius," (Hendricks, 2010). When you experience more positivity, happiness, or success than you're comfortable with, you trigger your "upper limit switch," thus, bringing you back down to your old comfort level, (Hendricks, 2010). In other words, you create negativity that makes the positive feelings short-lived. This puts you right back in your old "box."

I decided to spend my weekend getting myself prepared to stay in my Zone of Genius. I started by reading the last three chapters of the book that covered how to do this and another new concept called "Einstein Time." Hendricks' theory on Einstein Time is that each person is her own source of time. You create a new relationship with time by not looking at it as finite or scarce. Instead, you have to believe you always have enough time to do what matters in each moment. It was a complete paradigm shift for me.

After finishing the book, I decided I would now live my next journey on my own timeline. I would keep all the components I felt were needed in my ideal day but do them without worrying about when they were being done. If something came up, I would still make time in my day to accomplish everything I needed.

I began my second week of corporate freedom with this new realization. It was a complete 180-degree shift from my first week. The only two times of my day that mattered were 6 a.m. and 2 p.m. since both involved getting Alice to and from school. Other than that, everything else that I deemed necessary would get done, regardless of the time.

Finishing this book and training for the marathon were my two biggest priorities. I kept all the other components that I had listed in my ideal day but without any of the times. I miraculously got everything done that I needed to each day.

I felt *amazing!*

My energy was higher than I had felt in years, and I even started to present myself differently, physically. I dressed in clothes that weren't meant for workouts. I did my hair and makeup. I finished revisions on six chapters, sent my introduction and chapter one to my beta readers for feedback on my writing, and finished raising the rest of my goal for publishing fees. I accomplished *massive* action.

Finding Your Ritual

Each of my daily rituals is just a small piece, but when added together and practiced daily, have a big impact on my emotional energy and daily stability. The important thing is that each of them brought me joy and was selected for that reason. I have a consistent balance of mind, body, and spirit practices. It's my daily happiness recipe.

I no longer have a timeline. I know I am the source of my time and will be able to get everything done. I am able to live in my Zone of Genius so that I can live my purpose and help others find stability with their mental health.

What little pieces can you put together and practice each day to make sure you have "me" time, along with a balance of mind, body, and soul? What does your personal happiness recipe look like? Are you the source of your time? Create your ideal day and live in your joy and success.

CHAPTER 14

THE KEY: MIND, BODY & SPIRIT

"Happiness can be found even in the darkest of times, if one only remembers to turn on the light."

—ALBUS DUMBLEDORE

Every day is different. No one day will be the same as any other. It's taken me a long time, but I've discovered that I need my own personal happiness recipe. It allows me to thrive and find stability with bipolar disorder.

What I have learned is essential. The balance consists of three key parts: mind, body, and spirit. When I have a day that's full of each, I am at my happiest. The key is realizing you are in control of your own happiness.

If you go for weeks only focusing on intense exercise, you'll find yourself depleted physically and mentally exhausted. If you fall off the wagon with your diet for weeks on end, you'll find your body sluggish and your energy low. Without self-love or long periods away from nature, you'll feel an internal depletion.

It doesn't have to be the same plan every day. Life happens. Mood swings happen. Some days, I do everything in my power but can't quite shake the darkness. On other days, all I need is my morning smoothie and a quick walk around the block to balance myself.

You can use as few or as many techniques as you need each day. It's entirely up to you. That is the beauty of having your own personal happiness plan. All you need is a list of things that bring you joy that you can activate:

Start by labeling three columns at the top of a piece of paper "mind," "body," and "soul," respectively. Close your eyes, take a deep, long breath and ask yourself, "What could I do that would bring me joy and nourish my mind?"

- Open your eyes and start writing whatever answers come to mind. Let the words flow, absent of any internal judgment.

- Repeat the process, replacing "body" and then "soul" at the end of the question. Once you have your completed lists, read each column and star any response that brings a smile or causes a spark inside you. Let your inner voice guide you.

- Take two or three of the starred responses from each column and write out your own personal happiness plan. You can keep it in your journal, decorate it on paper and hang it on your mirror, or make it a daily reminder on your phone.

I have mine in a notebook on my desk open to that page in order to reference whenever I need it. It is also a picture favorited on my phone, in case I'm not at home. Start by incorporating at least one aspect from each of the three areas into your daily routine. Remember, use as many or as few as you need every day; just make sure to incorporate a balance of mind, body, and spirit.

- It is also important to identify your own support system. Who do you have in your life that you can reach out to whenever needed? Your support system should be comprised of individuals who are great listeners and can come from a place without judgment. They don't need to have prior experience; they just need to be able to support you and hear you during the bad times and the good. Keep in mind that pets can be on this list too.

Write a list of those in your support system at the top of your happiness plan. Don't hesitate to ask them to be accountability partners while you establish your new rituals and routines. Invite them to participate with you in your daily body practice, like taking a walk or going to the gym to exercise. Share a playlist you created on a music app with them. You do not have to go on this journey alone.

Lesson Learned

Writing this book wasn't as easy as I thought it might be. It went pretty well for the first few months, but as fall turned into winter and COVID-19 continued to alter our lives as we knew it, it became a mind game for me to force myself to write something.

As the weeks went on, my progress ground to a halt. Roadblock after roadblock impeded any forward progress, to the point of feeling like there was absolutely nothing more I could do. I felt that I would finally lose my stability and be forced back onto medication while writing a book designed to inspire others on how to thrive in a life with mental illness!

What I learned from this period of time, though, was that the universe never gives you more than you can handle. I had lessons I needed to learn and more phases in my growth before I would be ready for my next chapter in life. I came across a quote by Gabby Bernstein a few days ago that perfectly sums up the lesson:

> "When you ask the universe to go to the next level, don't be surprised if things fall apart first. Consider it a good sign."

My struggles helped me to build the mental strength that would be required to take massive action towards big changes in my life. Coping with my job had me out of alignment in my balance of mind, body, and spirit. It wasn't supporting me on my path to fulfill my purpose, and my self-confidence had taken a major blow. The kick in the butt from my psychiatrist and the love from my coach and support system allowed me to put a plan in place to move forward towards my next chapter in life.

In September 2021, I left my job in the corporate world and recommitted to my daily rituals. I designed a new personal happiness recipe, began training for a full marathon, and started eating plant-based regularly. My favorite music was my constant companion while I dove into revisions for this book, making sure to take breaks to rest in my hammock or the rocking chair on my back porch.

I went for hikes at the nearby Pedernales Falls State Park with Tony on his weekdays off and booked a long weekend trip to Colorado to catch the Aspen leaves changing colors. I participated in an eight-week-long group coaching program so that I can launch my coaching practice at the start of 2022 in order to help others find joy and stability with their mental health through mind, body, and spirit practices.

I lived and breathed the lessons I had learned in the past few years on my spiritual journey, and everything shifted again. I weighed the same, but my body looked different. My side profile noticeably slimmed after just a week, almost as if I had liposuction around my lower abdomen.

I was full of energy and enthusiastic about spending hours working on revisions for this book every day. Listening to a new audiobook during my marathon training sessions inspired me to research and develop a coaching method to help others reduce or eliminate medications for their mental illness. My mood was highly anabolic, and I felt my emotional energy continue to rise every day. I was living my ideal day, on repeat, and thriving.

My lessons are simple and can be easily applied and incorporated into your life. Stability is possible with a mental illness, and you can learn to thrive in your life with it as well.

Bipolar disorder no longer defines me. It has allowed me to grow in ways I would never have been able to. I have learned so much about who Kate Arredondo really is while on my spiritual journey finding stability without medication. I now know what my purpose in this life is and how strong I truly am.

I reflect on the night I so nearly ended it all and have nothing but gratitude for the moments I have been able to have since then. There was, and is, so much more life to live.

My ultimate vision is to one day be able to sit on my cabin porch overlooking the Rocky Mountains and watch the mountain peaks light up in rosy hues of pinks and purples with every sunrise. I will have found the alpenglow, my daily dose of the divine light.

Until then, I will keep living, growing, and thriving.

For those of you on a journey to stability, what is your next step?

You are strong.

Be brave.

Take a deep breath.

You are worth it.

You can thrive.

"Long, blue, spiky-edged shadows crept out across the snow-fields, while a rosy glow, at first scarce discernible, gradually deepened and suffused every mountain-top, flushing the glaciers and the harsh crags above them. This was the alpenglow, to me the most impressive of all the terrestrial manifestations of God. At the touch of this divine light, the mountains seemed to kindle to a rapt, religious consciousness, and stood hushed like devout worshippers waiting to be blessed."

—JOHN MUIR

ACKNOWLEDGEMENTS

I am forever grateful to family and friends who supported me on my book-writing journey so that I could turn a fifteen-year-old dream into a reality.

A huge shout out to my husband for loving and believing in me. I appreciate you giving me all the time I needed over the last year so that I could write without interruption. To my daughter, for giving me the gift of motherhood and quietly playing during workshops and phone calls.

I am especially thankful for my parents, who always support me in whatever I do. To my mother who used her expertise to diligently read, edit and polish my very rough draft. To my brother and sister, who were always available for long phone calls and words of wisdom.

To all my pets, who share their gift of unconditional love with me.

I appreciate the professionals in my life who hold space for others to release and heal:

> My psychiatrist—Dr. Michele Hauser
> My coach—Lauren Bryant
> My iPEC colleagues and coaches

Thank you to my community of supporters who graciously contributed to my publishing campaign so that I could share my book with the world.

Angell Delgado

Ashley Felt

Ashton Nast

Blake Baumann

Brad Keeter

Brittany Slovak

Caitlyn Thibodeaux

Cathy Nairn

Chad Morgan

Chris Duran

Chris Ortiz

Courtney Villasenor

Diane Tucker

Gabriela Baeza

George Turner

Jacob Pacheco

Janie Good

Joel Peck

Jonathan Kay

Joseph Arredondo

Joseph Cummins

Julie Willis

Lauren Bryant

Lidia Flores

Lisa Boehnke

Maegan Dominguez

Marcia Van Brunt

Melanie Kimberlin

Nancy Turner

Natalie Good

Oscar Vazquez

Patsy Turner

Rachel Leach

Richard Sanders

Robert Sanders

Robert L Turner Jr.

Sam Turner

Sergey Kochergan

Tessa Lawton

The Hodsons

Thank you to the teams at New Degree Press and the Creator Institute for your patience and guidance in helping an accountant turn into an author. I would especially like to thank Eric Koester, Brian Bies, and my amazing editors, Alayna Eberhart, Cameron Alexander, Amanda Munro, and Shawna Quigley.

APPENDIX

______

Introduction

Centers for Disease Control and Prevention. "About Mental Health."
Last reviewed June 28, 2021. https://www.cdc.gov/mentalhealth/
learn/index.htm

Chapter 2

Curtin, Melanie. "Neuroscience Says Listening to This Song
Reduces Anxiety by Up to 65 Percent: Sure to both stir your
soul and calm your nervous system." *Inc.,* May 30, 2017.
https://www.inc.com/melanie-curtin/neuroscience-says-listen-
ing-to-this-one-song-reduces-anxiety-by-up-to-65-percent.html
Heshmat, Shahram. "Music, Emotion, and Well-Being: How does
music affect the way we think, feel, and behave?" *Psychology
Today,* August 25, 2019. https://www.psychologytoday.com/ca/
blog/science-choice/201908/music-emotion-and-well-being

Karpas, Patricia. *"How Music Helps You Heal."* Interview with Jim Donovan. *Untangle.* The Meditation Studio. September 29, 2020. Episode 277. Podcast audio, 51:14. https://soundcloud.com/untangle/jim-donovan-how-music-helps-you-heal

Psychology Today. "What Is Memory?" Reviewed by *Psychology Today* Staff. Accessed January 12, 2021. https://www.psychologytoday.com/ca/basics/memory

RawVolume. *"15 Years Ago, Music Helped Heal a Nation During 9/11."* September 7, 2016. http://rawvolume.com/15-years-music-heal-911/

Sachs, Matthew, Robert Ellis, Gottfied Schlaug, Psyche Loui. "Brain connectivity reflects human aesthetic responses to music." *Social Cognitive and Affective Neuroscience.* March 10, 2016. 11. nsw009. 10.1093/scan/nsw009. https://www.researchgate.net/publication/297744120_Brain_connectivity_reflects_human_aesthetic_responses_to_music

Soni, Akanksha. "Top 20 Songs to Help With Depression and Anxiety." *Calm Sage.* August 2, 2021. https://www.calmsage.com/songs-to-help-with-depression-and-anxiety/

Spielberg, Robin. "The Healing Power of Music." Filmed June 6, 2014 at TEDxLancaster, Lancaster, PA. Video, 21:30. https://youtu.be/8LTusPwrH9E

Thompson, Megan, Melanie Saltzman. "Why music has such profound effects on the brain." Interview with Indre Viskontas. September 29, 2019. Produced by PBS. Video, 5:04. https://www.pbs.org/newshour/show/why-music-has-such-profound-effects-on-the-brain

Chapter 3

Tyler, Jake. "I'm Fine—Learning to Live With Depression." Filmed October 2017 at TEDxBrighton. Brighton, East Sussex, United Kingdom. Video, 16:04. https://www.ted.com/talks/jake_tyler_i_m_fine_learning_to_live_with_depression

Chapter 4

Hölzel, Britta K, James Carmody, Mark Vangel, et al. "Mindfulness practice leads to increases in regional brain gray matter density." *Psychiatry Res* 191, no. 1 (2011): 36-43. https://www.ncbi.nlm.nih.gov/pmc/articles/PMC3004979/

TCMS Physician Wellness Program. "The Effects of Mindfulness Meditation on Medical Conditions." Presented by Michele Hauser, MD. October 10, 2020. Video, 33:29. https://youtu.be/r_iXjefQobY

Ying, Yang, Wang Jian-Zhi. "From Structure to Behavior in Basolateral Amygdala-Hippocampus Circuits." *Frontiers in Neural Circuits* 11, (2017): 86. https://www.frontiersin.org/articles/10.3389/fncir.2017.00086/full

Chapter 5

Fulkerson, Lee, John Corry, Joey Aucoin, Neal D. Barnard, and Gene Baur. 2011. *Forks over knives.* New York: Virgil Films.

Institute for Optimum Nutrition. "Mood food: How nutrition affects your mental health." Adapted from Optimum Nutrition Winter 2019/20. https://www.ion.ac.uk/news/mood-food-how-nutrition-affects-your-mental-health

Robertson, Ruairi. "Food for thought: How your belly controls your brain." Filmed December 2015 at TEDxFulbrightSanta-Monica. Santa Monica, CA. Video, 14:30. https://youtu.be/awtmTJW9ic8

Selhub, Eva "Nutritional psychiatry: Your brain on food." Harvard Health Publishing. March 26, 2020. https://www.health.harvard.edu/blog/nutritional-psychiatry-your-brain-on-food-201511168626

Chapter 6

Gingell, Sarah. "How Your Mental Health Reaps the Benefits of Exercise: New research shows why physical exercise is essential to mental health." *Psychology Today*. Reviewed by Ekua Hagan. March 22, 2018. https://www.psychologytoday.com/us/blog/what-works-and-why/201803/how-your-mental-health-reaps-the-benefits-exercise

Chapter 7

American Psychological Association. *"Stress effects on the body."* November 1, 2018. http://www.apa.org/topics/stress/body

Harvey AG, Kaplan KA, Soehner AM. "Interventions for Sleep Disturbance in Bipolar Disorder." *Sleep Med Clinics* 10, no. 1 (March 2015): 101-105. https://www.ncbi.nlm.nih.gov/pmc/articles/PMC4347516/

Chapter 8

Weir, Kirsten. "The roots of mental illness." *Monitor on Psychology* 43, no. 6. (June 2012): 30. http://www.apa.org/monitor/2012/06/roots

Chapter 12

Schneider, Bruce D. *Life & Leadership Potentials Training Workbook*, Institute for Professional Excellence in Coaching

Chapter 13

Hendricks, Gay. *The Big Leap: Conquer Your Hidden Fear and Take Life to the Next Level*. New York: HarperOne, 2010.